Family Devotional

Family Bible Study for Kids, Teens and Parents to Get Closer to God

By

Eileen Nyberg

ADISAN Publishing AB

TABLE OF CONTENTS

Introduction

Welcome to our family devotional for busy families. We recognize that in our modern day, families rarely have time to sit together at the dinner table. Lost are the days when this was a daily occurrence, therefore this devotional is designed to encourage you as a family, with your children, both young, and adolescent, to sit together at the dinner table at least two times a week.

Together, you will read a portion of scripture from the New Living Translation of the Bible. This is an easy-to-read and fairly simple translation for all ages to understand. Then you will together as a family look at the ideas, the discussion questions, and possible activities that you can do throughout your week.

By doing this, our goal is to cultivate a lifestyle that will allow your family's faith to become active. To realize that we are meant to do more than go to church and that devotions look differently for everyone. They are more than a brief reading at the beginning of your day. They can be put into action and spur you to mature faith in Christ.

We hope that these will draw you closer to God, but you will also become closer as a family. For in Ecclesiastes 4:12, the Bible tells us that a rope by itself may be "defeated, but two can stand back-to-back and conquer. Three are even better, for a triple-braided cord is not easily broken."

Our desire is for you and your family to be like that triple-braided rope. Wound together and bonded so tightly that you cannot be easily torn apart. We pray that God will also inspire you as a family to do His will, grow in His might, and experience His power's glory as you step out in faith.

"May God bless you and protect you. May the Lord smile on you and be gracious to you. May the Lord show you his favour and give you his peace."

Numbers 6:24-26

In The Beginning

CREATION

"In the beginning, God created the heavens and the earth."
- Genesis 1:1

Have you ever gone to the zoo and looked at the many different animals? There is the long-neck giraffe and the black and white striped zebra. How about looking into the clouds and seeing different shapes and sizes that look like objects or animals on earth? Maybe you have watched the sunset and watched as the many different colours appeared and disappeared. God has created all of that and so much more that we have yet to discover, including you. Plus, there is no one like you. You might find someone who looks similar but I can guarantee that your fingerprints and your character are unique. That makes God creative and that makes you one of a kind.

Talk about it: Discuss how each person in the family is different, and share with each other something you like about them.

Activity: Plan to go to the zoo or for a walk in nature. Look at the different varieties of animals and plants to notice how creative God is.

Prayer: Dear God, thank you for making every one of us unique. You care for us, and we thank you for making us. Amen.

THE FALL OF MAN

"When the cool evening breezes were blowing, the man and his wife heard the Lord God walking about in the garden. So they hid from the Lord God among the trees."
- Genesis 3:8

Have you ever done something wrong? Lied about not doing your homework or broke something in the house and then hid it from everyone else. I remember a time when I did something so bad, I hid under the bed. Nobody could find me and soon the whole neighbourhood was looking for me. I don't remember what I did wrong, but I sure had everyone worried. Adam and Eve did something similar. God told them not to eat from the tree in the middle of the garden, but a snake came along and showed them how delicious the fruit was. They ate from the tree and when God showed up, they hid. I'm sure God was worried about them too.

Talk About It: Take a moment to talk about when we do something wrong, that we shouldn't try and hide it. Express to each other that we will still love each other no matter what we do.

Activity: Organize a time to play, "Would You Rather." Give each other choices to make and ask, "Would you rather do __________ or __________? Make some questions serious and make other questions silly.

Prayer: Dear God, help us to not do wrong, but when we do, help us to look for help and not hide. Amen.

SIBLINGS FIGHT

One day Cain suggested to his brother, "Let's go out into the fields." And while they were in the field, Cain attacked his brother, Abel, and killed him.

- Genesis 4:8

Ever wanted to punch your brother or sister? That person made you so mad that you didn't want them in the house anymore. I got into a fight with my brother and my mom thought we were playing, so she got the camera and started taking pictures. We laugh about it today, but brothers and sisters fight. Thankfully we have never gotten so mad that we killed the other person. However, Cain was upset because he thought God loved Abel more. He didn't know that God was loving Abel the way he needed to be loved. Our parents might do the same. They may treat us differently because we don't act like the other person and we all need to be loved in our own way.

Talk About It: Tell a special or funny memory you had with your brother or sister and why you like it so much.

Activity: Take time in the week to make a family tree and talk about how special each and every family member is. Especially take the time to talk about brothers and sisters.

Prayer: Dear God, thank you for giving us, brothers and sisters. Help us to remember how special they are to us. Amen.

THE BIG FLOOD

I have placed my rainbow in the clouds. It is the sign of my covenant with you and with all the earth.

- Genesis 9:13

After a big storm and the sun begins to shine, have you ever looked outside to see if you can find a rainbow? If you do, look closely. You will see red, orange, yellow, green, blue, violet, and indigo. Each colour is special and it was created by God as a promise that he will never flood the earth with water again. Why would God flood the earth? He wanted to give us a second chance. People became so bad that he could only find one family in the world that loved him. So, he helped them build a big boat and survive the flood and then promised to never do it again. And he never has because God keeps his promises.

Talk About It: Was there ever a time when someone broke a promise to you? Discuss how that made you feel and how important it is to keep our promises.

Activity: During the week, see who can find the most rainbows. Every time you see a rainbow outside, on TV, or even on the computer, write down where you saw it. The person who finds the most wins.

Prayer: Dear God, thank you for keeping your promise to never flood the earth again. Also thank you for giving us a second chance. Amen.

BEING FAMOUS

I will make you into a great nation. I will bless you and make you famous, and you will be a blessing to others.

- Genesis 12:2

Imagine for a moment being a movie or a rock star. Maybe even a King or a Queen. We might think it would be great to be famous. Many people will surround you with cameras and want your autograph. God promised to make Abram famous, and he did. He made him the father of a nation. However, nobody ask for his autograph and nobody took his picture. He never became famous until many years after he died. To God, being famous is different than what we see on the screen. He wants to make you famous so that you can be a blessing to others.

Talk About It: Would you rather be a movie or rock star famous or would you want to be famous like Abram? Why?

Activity: As a family figure out what you can do to be a blessing to someone else. For example, donate to a food bank, make a meal for another family, or help clean someone else's yard.

Prayer: Dear God, help us to be famous like Abram. To be a blessing to others. Amen.

A CHEERFUL GIVER

"God will provide a sheep for the burnt offering, my son," Abraham answered. And they both walked on together.

- Genesis 22:8

God loves a cheerful giver. But there are times we don't want to give to God. For example, Abraham was asked to give God his son. He wasn't happy about it, but he decided to obey God. At just the last moment, God provided a sheep instead of his son. We are not always happy to give to God. To put money in the plate or the box at church, especially when we can use our money for something else. When we do, God will provide much as he provided for Abraham. He knows exactly what we need.

Talk About It: Discuss the importance of giving to your local church and how much God provides when we do. If you have a story of God's provision, share it with the family.

Activity: The Old Testament talks about tithing, or giving ten percent of everything you make. This week, do chores or work around the house for money and learn how to give ten percent.

Prayer: Thank you, God, for providing our food, clothing, and house. Help us to be cheerful in giving back to you. Amen.

A LOVE STORY

He loved her deeply, and she was a special comfort to him….
- Genesis 24:67

Do you ever think it is gross when two people kiss? Maybe you have seen it on tv and thought yuck. But imagine praying to God for that special person in your life. That one person that you want to kiss. That was Isaac. He prayed to God and he found Rebekah. He loved her so much, that he agreed to work seven years for her father in order to marry her. That seems like true love. God's love for us is more than a kiss. In fact, he gave up his one and only son so that we can one day live in heaven. Now that is so much better than kissing.

Talk About It: Explain the varieties of love a person can have. For example, one can love pizza, but one can also love a person. The greatest of these is the love God has for us and together try to figure out how that is different.

Activity: Put everyone's name on separate pieces of paper and have everyone draw one name. Take the time to make a card or write a letter explaining how that person is special to you and why you love them

Prayer: Thank you, God, for loving us. For giving up your one and only son so that we can one day live in heaven. Amen.

MORE SIBLINGS FIGHT

From that time on, Esau hated Jacob because their father had given Jacob the blessing. And Esau began to scheme: "I will soon be mourning my father's death. Then I will kill my brother, Jacob."

- Genesis 27:41

My sister used to chase me around the house, blowing a horn in my ear until our parents would make her stop. They would place the horn in their bedroom, and she would think of ways to sneak in and take it so she could chase me again. Have you ever thought of a way to annoy another person in the house? Esau wanted to do more than annoying; he wanted to kill his brother. However, God doesn't want us to annoy each other, and he especially doesn't want us to kill. Instead, he wants us to learn ways to help each other and learn how not to fight.

Talk about it: Find ways you can help one another as a family. Take this time to ask if someone needs help with something.

Activity: Draw names out of a hat and surprise that person by doing something special for them.

Prayer: Today God we ask you to help us to be less annoying and more helpful. May we be an encouragement to someone else. Amen.

A WRESTLING MATCH

This left Jacob all alone in the camp, and a man came and wrestled with him until the dawn began to break.

Wrestling takes a lot of work and many people train countless hours to try and go to Olympics. At the most, a wrestling match might last fifteen minutes before they determine who the winner is. Jacob wrestled all night because he didn't want to meet his brother. He must have been exhausted! This seems silly, but if we remember, Esau wanted to kill Jacob. So, it makes sense for him to wrestle with someone else. Instead, God wants us to be quick to forgive and not let the sun go down on our anger. So may we be more willing to talk to each other instead of wrestling with strangers.

Talk About It: Are there ways to talk to each other when someone is angry as a family? If you don't already have a system discuss a good way to not let the sun go down on someone's anger.

Activity: Here's a fun and silly game to play. Pillow Sumo Wrestling. Find a safe space in the house or outside. Stuff a couple of pillows up your shirts, take a running start and bump tummies. Whoever falls first loses. Sometimes, just being silly is a great way to connect.

Prayer: Thank you, God, for giving us feelings. Even when we are mad. Help us when we are mad, and help us to forgive others. Amen.

THE FAVOURITE CHILD

But his brothers hated Joseph because their father loved him more than the rest of them. They couldn't say a kind word to him.

- Genesis 37:4

Have you ever felt like mom and dad like your brother and sister better than you? If not, you are either an only child or you might be the favourite. Now, in reality, nobody is the favourite, and in the case of Joseph, he was treated differently because his dad was very old when he was born.

This might not seem like a good excuse, but he didn't have much time left and Joseph's dad wanted to make the most of every single moment. Unfortunately, this made Joseph's brothers mad, and they eventually sold him into slavery.

We might want to do that to one of our brothers and sisters. Instead, we need to talk about how we feel about mom and dad. Find out why it seems like the other person is the favourite, and let mom and dad explain why you might be treated differently than everyone else.

Talk About It: Discuss today's devotional. Do we feel like people in the family are treated differently? If so, explain why.

Activity: Spend one night this week doing something one child likes. Then spend the next night doing something another child wants to do, and keep investing in each child until they all get a turn.

Prayer: Thank you God for giving us each member of the family. You have no favourites and love each of us. Amen.

FORGIVENESS

You intended to harm me, but God intended it all for good. He brought me to this position so I could save the lives of many people.

- Genesis 50:20

In our last devotional, Joseph's brothers hated him and sold him into slavery. This should have made Joseph mad. Has anyone in the family ever made you mad? How did you react?

I'm sure Joseph was mad and confused at first. However, over time, Joseph learned to forgive. He even says, "God intended it all for good." Because eventually, Joseph became second in charge over a whole nation and was able to help his father and his brothers when there was no food.

Joseph could have spent his life mad at his brothers. Instead, he chooses to forgive. When someone in the family makes us mad, it's okay to be mad, but we need to learn to deal with our feelings and eventually forgive each other.

Talk About It: In the moments of our life, when someone makes us mad, what are some ways we can come up with to get past our feelings and learn to forgive?

Activity: This week, write a letter to someone else in the family. Make sure everyone gets to receive a letter. In the letter, write five things that make the person special and why you like them.

Prayer: Forgiving God, we thank you for giving us a second chance. Help us to do the same for others. Amen.

400 Years Later

MOSES

Later, when the boy was older, his mother brought him back to Pharaoh's daughter, who adopted him as her own son. The princess named him Moses, for she explained, "I lifted him out of the water."

- Exodus 2:10

After Joseph's family joined him in a new nation, the family grew and eventually, they became slaves. Four hundred years later, God decided it was time to free Joseph's family. He gave this job to Moses, someone who was found floating in a basket as a baby.

However, God knew that this baby was going to be special. He had a plan for his life, just like he has a plan for our lives. Because of that plan he had Moses lifted out of the water, and in the next few days we will learn more about how God changed his life.

Talk about it: God has a plan for your life. Discuss as a family if each person believes this is true. Why is this hard to believe or what do you think God's plan is for your life? How can the family help you with that plan?

Activity: Plans take time to unfold. As a family, take time to plan a dream vacation. Discover what is needed to make the trip a reality and discuss how long it will take to see it happen. What can each family member do to help?

Prayer: God, thank you for giving us dreams, and having a plan for our lives. Help us, learn about your dreams and your plans for our lives. Amen.

SANDALS AND BURNING BUSHES

"Do not come any closer," the Lord warned. "Take off your sandals, for you are standing on holy ground.

- Exodus 3:5

Have you ever taken your shoes off and felt the grass between your toes or even buried your feet in the sand on a beach? Sometimes it feels good to run around in your bare feet and God asked Moses to take his sandals off for he was on holy ground and standing in front of a burning bush.

The word 'holy' means to set apart and this moment in his life was extra special. God wanted to mark the occasion by asking him to stand on his bare feet. To be closer to God. To be a part of the event.

Today, many people don't get special moments like this with God. However, the Bible also tells us that if we come close to God, he will come close to us. So may we watch for our special moments with God.

Talk About It: Has anyone in the family had a special moment with God? It may seem like something small compared to a burning bush, but use your moment to encourage everyone else.

Activity: Find a nearby museum or cathedral and visit it. See if you can find special moments in history where God has inspired someone.

Prayer: Help us, Lord, to come close to you so that you might come close to us. Amen.

FROGS AND GNATS

Then the Lord said to Moses, "Go back to Pharaoh and announce to him, 'This is what the Lord says: Let my people go, so they can worship me.

Frogs make a ribbit sound, and sometimes they make a purrreeek sound at night. Gnats are like mosquitos and they make a buzzing noise, but at the moment God wanted to free his people, he sent other animals to encourage Pharaoh. He also sent flies and locusts.

These animals are okay, but in huge groups, they can be annoying and cause a lot of damage. It still wasn't enough to make Pharaoh set God's people free. He still wanted more and sometimes we can be greedy like Pharaoh.

It doesn't matter how annoying our brother or sister may be. We still want our way. But both Pharaoh and God's people weren't happy. The same can be said of us and how everyone else can be sad when one person tries to get their way.

Talk About It: Has anyone ever had a temper tantrum? How did it make the rest of the family feel? Was there a better solution and what might it be and why?

Activity: Go to a nearby pet store that has frogs, crickets, and other bugs. Imagine together what it would be like if there were thousands of them and discover how stubborn Pharaoh was.

Prayer: Heavenly Father, help us to be mindful of other people. Help us not to have temper tantrums. Amen.

MOVING DAY

Pharaoh sent for Moses and Aaron during the night. "Get out!" he ordered. "Leave my people—and take the rest of the Israelites with you! Go and worship the Lord as you have requested.

- Exodus 12:31

Has mom and dad ever announced that you had to move to a new town or a new school? Nobody wants to move, but sometimes it is necessary. It might be because mom or dad got a new job or your school is closing.

It might be exciting going to a new place, but we might also be sad because of all the people we will miss. In the case of Moses, he would have been both excited and sad. He was excited because they would finally be free, but he was sad because Pharaoh only gave him one night to pack and move.

Regardless of why people are moving, it is sometimes a part of life and there is nothing we can do about it. We have to make the best of the moment and realize that no matter where we go, God is with us.

Talk About It: Have you ever moved? What do you miss about the last place? Has someone you know moved? What do you miss about them?

Activity: Plan a camping trip (maybe to the backyard or even a blanket fort in the house). What will you need to pack and how long will you be gone? Then go and have fun as a family.

Prayer: Thank you, God. It doesn't matter where we are. You are there. You never leave us. Amen.

SIGHTSEEING

So the people of Israel walked through the middle of the sea on dry ground, with walls of water on each side!

- Exodus 14:22

Ever go sightseeing? Remember all of the beautiful and amazing sights. I'm sure it would be hard to compare it to the sight of walking through the middle of the sea on dry ground. To see walls of water on both sides and to maybe even see a fish or two swimming higher than your head.

However, Pharaoh changed his mind. He didn't want Moses and his people to move. So he chased them and when Moses had nowhere to go, God parted the middle of the sea and the people got to walk across on dry ground. How cool is that? I'm sure it is a sight that none of them would ever forget.

Talk About It: What is the most amazing sight that everyone has seen? Let each person describe it.

Activity: Explore new places as a family. Maybe you can't afford to go somewhere that someone wants to go to. See if you can find a tour of the place online or in a book and discover the many sights for people to see.

Prayer: You do amazing things and we ask that you help us to see your wonders every day. May we be sightseers of your great miracles. Amen.

10 Rules

OTHER GODS

You must not have any other god but me.

- Exodus 20:3

God made ten rules for his people to follow. He did this because he loves us and he wants to protect us. This first rule is special because sometimes people want a different god in their life. One that maybe wouldn't make so many rules.

At times we might think someone else has better parents than their mom or dad. Maybe they give better gifts or a bigger allowance. It is easier to think that and it was easy for them to think that other gods were better than their God.

The problem is, that there is no other God. Only one God could truly help them, so God made the rule because he did not want them to fall into the trap of believing something was better when it wasn't.

Talk About It: Our parents are not gods, but they also provide for us. Think of all the ways your parents provide for you. Even if you are a parent remember everything your parents did for you and then express thanks for them.

Activity: As a family, set a financial budget, to help set realistic expectations instead of comparing your family to other families.

Prayer: Thank you, God, for being caring and loving. Help us not to compare you to others. Amen.

IDOLS

You must not make for yourself an idol of any kind or an image of anything in the heavens or on the earth or in the sea.

- Exodus 20:4

It might seem silly to make an animal out of wood or to take a baseball and worship it, but when this verse was written people did that. These objects didn't provide for them like God, but for some reason, they thought it was a good idea.

Now, we might not do that, but we might worship Ed Sheeran or Justin Bieber. We don't do it by carving an image out of wood. Instead, we spend a lot of our time listening to their music and buying clothing with their image on it. We spend more time doing that than we do worshipping God and that makes them idols.

We should be careful to make sure God comes first in our life. To spend more time reading his word or listening to worship music than listening to the tunes of Sheeran or Bieber.

Talk About It: Besides music, talk as a family about the different ways we can make idols in our lives.

Activity: As a family, chart how much time you worship God together and as individuals. Then compare that to the amount of time you watch television or spend listening to music that doesn't worship God. Find out if changes need to be made.

Prayer: Forgive us, God, if we have idols in our life. Help us to see and hear from you above all else. Amen.

You must not misuse the name of the Lord your God. The Lord will not let you go unpunished if you misuse his name.

- Exodus 20:7

Ever heard the phrase, "the old man upstairs"? Sometimes people refer to God as the old man upstairs sitting in his rocking chair. This doesn't make sense, for God is not an old man, which makes the statement disrespectful.

Other people will say, "Jesus Christ" or "Oh my God", and that is not referring to God. This is also disrespectful. Imagine talking about a person, pretending they are not there, when they are in the room, looking at you and even listening to you. That is what it is like to misuse God's name.

I'm sure it would hurt your feelings if you were the person being talked about. It also hurts God's feelings, and all he asks is that we don't misuse his name.

Talk About It: See who can find the following verses the fastest and then discuss the importance of God's name. Psalm 30:4, Romans 10:13, and Colossians 3:17.

Activity: This week, practice keeping God's name holy and see how you do. As a family, discuss when you make a mistake, and help one another to keep God's name holy through our words and our actions.

Prayer: Help us Heavenly Father to keep your name holy and special. Forgive us when we make a mistake and know that we love you. Amen.

SABBATH

Remember to observe the Sabbath day by keeping it holy.

- Exodus 20:8

Ever have a phone or a tablet needing a recharge? Of course, you have. Almost every single day, certain devices in our house need to be plugged in. They essentially need a rest.

We are the same. We need time to rest and that's why we sleep at night. However, there are times we need to even rest throughout the day. To recharge ourselves.

Now, we, of course, God didn't install batteries inside of us, but he did make us and he knows that we need rest. Therefore, he told us to remember to observe the Sabbath, a day of rest, and when we do this, we keep one day of the week holy, and our bodies are recharged.

Talk About It: Discuss a moment in your life when you were tired. Each person takes a turn. Then talk about ways each of you can rest.

Activity: Decide on a day this week to pretend it is a rainy day outside. Without leaving the house, spend some time with God, but also get out the board games and have indoor fun as a family.

Prayer: Dear God, thank you for making us, and thank you for giving us a day of rest. Help us to honour that day and make it special. Amen.

PARENTS

Honour your father and mother. Then you will live a long, full life in the land the Lord your God is giving you.

- Exodus 20:12

What are some of the rules in your house? Clean your room, do your homework, and take out the garbage, no fighting or biting. Maybe you don't like the rules. I don't always either. But you know what? Honouring our parents is very important.

Part of our verse today says that we will live a long and full life if we honour our parents. Our parents set boundaries for us so that we won't get hurt and when we stepped outside of them we could get into big trouble. Therefore, if we want to survive in life and win, then we should listen to our parents and honour them.

Talk About It: What are some of the rules at home that are easy to obey? Which ones are harder to obey? Do the adults in the home have rules? What are they? Discuss the importance of rules.

Activity: Help each other around the house. What are some chores that mom and dad have to do and what are some chores that the children have to do? Is there one thing we can do to help someone else make their job easier?

Prayer: Dear God, thank you for our parents. Teach us to honour them with our service. Amen.

VALUE LIFE

Now, not many of us will kill another person. It is even law and even when people don't follow God, they can agree that killing people is bad. However, this rule is also about how we should value life.

Ever seen someone help a turtle cross the road? Maybe you have seen people on television talking about animals and their importance to the planet. Sometimes we value life by trying to recycle or making sure we use fewer plastics.

Valuing life means that we must not murder, but it also means that we should do what we can to help keep the beautiful planet that God gave us. So may we do our part to make life on earth better for ourselves and the animals around us.

Talk About It: Just imagine if you made a beautiful painting and then someone came and tore it in half. Discuss how it feels for God if we don't take care of his creation and some ways that we can value life.

Activity: As a family, spend part of the day, cleaning up along the side of the road. Discover all the trash people throw out of their cars and discuss the importance of keeping things clean.

Prayer: Help us God to value the life you have created. May we learn how to keep the planet clean. Amen.

ADULTERY

You must not commit adultery.

- Exodus 20:14

Many of us will fall in love and get married someday, so it is important to know that after we get married, we can't like anyone else the same as our spouse. We even make a promise to the other person that we won't.

Promises are important and they should be kept. Remember Noah's Ark and how God kept his promise never to flood the world again? Adults, after getting married, need to try and keep their promises to each other.

Now, this rule is for adults, but we can learn to follow this when we are young. We can learn to keep our promises. When we say we are going to do something, we should make sure we do it.

Talk About It: Why is it important for us to keep our promises? Why do you think marriage is so important to God?

Activity: Make a family tree and talk about the good and bad historical parts of the family. Discuss how people make mistakes and how we need to learn to forgive and still love them.

Prayer: Thank you God for your goodness to me. Please help me to always keep my promises. Amen.

STEALING

You must not steal.

- Exodus 20:15

Usually, when we think of stealing, we think of a bad guy wearing a mask, or robbing a bank. If you think about it, there are many ways to break this rule.

What about taking a toy and hiding it from your brother or sister? Maybe you just took something because you wanted it, but you planned to return it when you were done. Ever wonder how the other person felt? Chances are, they were worried since they couldn't find whatever they were looking for.

When we steal, it hurts other people. When we do something to hurt others, we are not respecting them. So the command to not steal is a command to protect other people's stuff and to make sure they don't get hurt. It is common to respect and care for others.

Talk About It: Are there other ways to steal? Discuss how it is possible to steal time and ideas or how you can steal someone's reputation through gossip.

Activity: Take the opportunity this week to give or share a surprise hug or kiss with each other.

Prayer: Father God, you have given us everything we need. Help us to be content with what we have. Amen.

LYING

You must not testify falsely against your neighbour.

- Exodus 20:16

Ever tell someone the clothes they are wearing look nice, but you just don't want to hurt their feelings so you lie. It's just a small white lie or a tiny fib. No big deal. However, they can become a big deal.

On a big talent show that was being shown on television for the whole world to see a person got up to sing. She was horrible at singing and the judges told her so. However, she believed she was the greatest singer in the world because her mom had told her that every day.

God wants us to be honest, and we shouldn't bend the truth, even just a little. When we tell the truth we are helping the person, therefore we should find ways to do so in nice and loving ways.

Talk About It: Go around the room and talk about one thing each person should improve on. After that go around the room and make sure everyone knows something good about themselves.

Activity: Set up a mock trial with a judge. The case is about a missing cookie. Have one person try and defend themselves and see how hard it is to lie.

Prayer: Dear God, help us to tell the truth even when it is hard. Amen.

I WANT THAT!

You must not covet your neighbour's house. You must not covet your neighbour's wife, male or female servant, ox or donkey, or anything else that belongs to your neighbour.

- Exodus 20:17

Ever want that video game system that your friend has or maybe the big doll house in the store? Maybe it's a dirt bike or some stylish clothes. It just never seems to be enough. We always seem to want one thing more.

It becomes so easy to want what we don't have and those desires can easily fill our hearts. This is what it means to covet. As we get older the objects get bigger and bigger and they cost more money. It's hard to keep up; therefore the sooner we learn to be satisfied with what we have, the better we will be later on in life.

Talk About It: Begin to make a dream list of everything you want that you don't have. Discuss why we can't have it all and the importance of being happy with what we got. Even talk about the items you have but don't use anymore.

Activity: Collect the items in your house that you don't use anymore and then find a place to donate them so that someone else can use them.

Prayer: Help us, God, to be happy with what we have and not desire the things we don't have. Amen.

Weird Laws

GOD LIKES SALT

Season all your grain offerings with salt to remind you of God's eternal covenant. Never forget to add salt to your grain offerings.

- Leviticus 2:13

We season our food with salt and the bible even talks about how we shouldn't lose our saltiness. It also becomes apparent that God seems to like his salt. He wants his grain offerings seasoned with salt to remind the people of God's eternal covenant.

This might seem a little odd, but salt was widely used to preserve their meat. At the same time, it was a symbol of loyalty and friendship, therefore God wanted them to use salt as a way to express the need to preserve their relationship.

Which, we can now look at this weird law in a different light. Instead of telling God that he might want to skip the salt shaker on the table, we can now realize that God was attempting to preserve his friendship with the people of Israel.

Talk About It: Discuss some of the friends each of you have and how important they are to you.

Activity: Over the next couple of days invite some of your friends over for dinner or a board game night. Continue to deepen your relationships with them.

Prayer: Thank you, God, for wanting to continue your friendship with us. Help us to return the favour. Amen.

CARELESS PROMISES

Or suppose you make a foolish vow of any kind, whether its purpose is for good or for bad. When you realize its foolishness, you must admit your guilt.

Has anyone in the family ever made you upset? Did they take your favourite toy or promise to do something and then never really do it? I'm sure it made you mad, and sometimes you might make yourself so mad that you promise to hurt them.

Now, we know you don't mean it, and God calls these foolish vows. When we calm down and realize what we have said, God wants us to go back to the person and say we are sorry. Overall, this isn't a weird law. Instead, this is a law that we should try to live out in our everyday lives.

Being the first to be sorry is a good thing. Even if we haven't done anything wrong, it will help us in building our relationships with others and overall it will make us better people.

Talk About It: Share some of your embarrassing stories with one another of how you got mad and said silly things that you regret. Did anyone say sorry and how did it make you feel?

Activity: Plan a quiet evening together as a family. Maybe watch a movie together or find a shared activity that everyone likes to do.

Prayer: In our moments when we are upset, help us God to watch what we say. When we mess up, help us to be the first to say sorry. Amen.

UNHOLY FIRE

So fire blazed forth from the Lord's presence and burned them up, and they died there before the Lord.

- Leviticus 10:2

Ever get bored in church? Wanted to sneak out of the room when everyone was singing or maybe just take a quick nap when no one was looking. Sometimes, we just come to church a little bit tired, so imagine if someone did something wrong and they died in the middle of the service because of it.

Now that would make people pay attention and that is exactly what happened to Nadab and Abihu. They decided to try and change things up in church and they died. Today, this would not happen, but sometimes churches have certain traditions for certain reasons and we should take the time to discover why.

Talk About It: Take a moment to discuss certain aspects of the church that others may not understand. Make sure everyone realizes that there are no dumb questions. Finish off by talking about the importance of going to church as a family.

Activity: This week at church, make a list of traditions or things that you do all the time. Maybe even invite the pastor and his/her family to dinner and ask about the importance of the church to them.

Prayer: Dear God. May we realize the importance of your church and help us to figure out how we should worship you. Amen.

MESSY HAIR

Do not show grief by leaving your hair uncombed…

- Leviticus 10:6

Before going to church, it seems like we always have to brush our hair and look presentable. Some churches still have people come in suits and dresses, while other churches seem to be okay with being a little bit more casual. Overall, brushing your hair seems to be important in all of them.

Now, this isn't a weird law about making sure you brush your hair before going to church. Instead, it is about making yourself look presentable before you go to a funeral. It also seems that God just wants us to try and look our best, even in moments when we just don't feel like it.

Therefore, it is okay to have a good pyjama day and lounge around the house. In those moments don't brush your hair. However, it does seem that when we leave the house, God would like you to pick up that comb and give your hair a quick brush.

Talk About It: Does this seem like a silly rule or how does everyone feel about God caring how we look?

Activity: Plan a pyjama day. Nobody leaves the house and everyone just takes a day to spend with the family.

Prayer: Thank you, for caring about us. Help us, to learn to care for ourselves in respectful ways. Amen.

HAM SANDWICHES

The pig has evenly split hooves but does not chew the cud, so it is unclean.

- Leviticus 11:7

Thick slices of ham with some cheese and mayonnaise or maybe some mustard between two slices of bread. This makes my mouth water and yet God made a rule that Jews couldn't eat the meat from a pig. He called them unclean.

Now, this isn't because pigs roll in the mud, nor did it have anything to do with the idea that pigs will eat anything. God wanted his people to be a bit different from the rest of the world, and therefore he said, "No pork chops, no bacon, and no ham sandwiches."

Later on, in the New Testament, God changed the rule. Today, we can enjoy a nice big ham sandwich with all the lunch meat we want on it. However, he still calls us to be different and it's up to us to figure out how.

Talk About It: Are there ways we are already different? Take a moment to discuss the differences between someone who goes to church and someone who doesn't.

Activity: Go through old pictures of the family. See if you can spot the differences between when the photos were taken and today.

Prayer: God, you have called us to be different from the world. Help us to do so. Amen.

DON'T TOUCH THE GRAPES

…do not pick up the grapes that fall to the ground.

- Leviticus 19:10

Ever heard of the five-second rule? If a piece of food falls to the ground, you have five seconds to pick it up. When you get it within that amount of time, you are good to eat it. Now, of course, some people think that is gross because the ground is dirty and even our kitchen floors are not the cleanest.

One might think that God is saying that there is no five-second rule, but they would be wrong. Instead, God is asking that the grapes that have fallen to the ground be given to the poor or people who don't have enough food. He doesn't want anything to be wasted and he wants everyone to have enough food to eat.

Talk About It: Have you ever seen a homeless person or someone begging for money on the side of the road? How did that make you feel and what are some ways that you can help?

Activity: As a family, gather up some food in the house or go to the grocery store and purchase some food to give to a food bank. When at the food bank, take the time to ask them how this helps other families and what it means to them.

Prayer: Thank you, God, for providing us with food. Help us, to help others. Amen.

POLYESTER AND COTTON

Do not wear clothing woven from two different kinds of thread.

- Leviticus 19:19

Look at the tag on your shirt. It probably has a combination of polyester and cotton. Most of our clothing is made that way and yet God told the Israelites that they could not wear clothes with two different kinds of thread.

Now, this does seem like an interesting and weird law. What does it matter to God what we wear as long as we are wearing clothes? Remember God wanted his people to be different from the rest of the world.

For us, we might buy a Christian t-shirt that has the name of Jesus written in big bold letters. Or maybe we will wear a necklace with a cross pennant on it. Overall, it is no longer wrong to wear clothes from two different kinds of thread, but maybe we should find ways to look different.

Talk About It: Today, we don't typically follow this rule and you might be able to find people who dress differently than you. Discuss some of the different styles of clothing you see.

Activity: Have a fashion show. Find the most outrageous and funny clothes you can find and then show them off to the rest of the family. The one who gets the most laughs wins.

Prayer: May we be people who respect you God with the clothes that we wear. Forgive us when we don't. Amen.

EATING FRUIT TOO SOON

When you enter the land and plant fruit trees, leave the fruit unharvested for the first three years and consider it forbidden. Do not eat it.

- Leviticus 19:23

God seems to have lost his mind. Why would anyone leave fruit hanging on a tree for three years? This seems like a waste, but we also live with microwaves and fast-food drive-thrus. We want everything now, but God was trying to teach the idea that good things come to those who wait.

If a person eats the fruit from a tree too early, the fruit hasn't had time to mature. The juices inside won't have time to sweeten or be full of flavour. Instead, the person will be missing out on the full experience of everything God wanted us to have, therefore we should wait.

Talk About It: How hard is it to wait? Take some time to discuss moments that we have trouble waiting for. Is it better to wait?

Activity: Try and go a week without something. It might be the television, a video game, or a certain kind of food. Help one another and find out how hard it is to wait for something that you want.

Prayer: Thank you God for teaching us the goodness behind waiting. Help us to be people who wait for good things to come. Amen.

DON'T TRIM YOUR BEARD

The priests must not shave their heads or trim their beards…

- Leviticus 21:5

Ever watched Duck Dynasty? The Robertson family is full of men who don't shave their heads or trim their beards. They seem to be a lot of fun, and they even pray before every meal but notice God didn't make this a requirement for everyone. He made this rule for priests.

Some of God's laws were made for specific people, and today we place different rules for our pastors and priests. We sometimes expect them to be better than others, but we should also remember that they are only human and just like us they make mistakes.

Today, God has made us all priests and he doesn't give us all of the same rules as he did in the Old Testament. We also shouldn't place too many expectations on the leaders of our churches. Instead, we should do all that we can to help them.

Talk About It: Discuss the importance of church leaders and ways that we can help them.

Activity: As a family, schedule an appointment with your pastor and find out if there are different expectations and rules for them.

Prayer: We thank you God for giving us, church leaders. Help us to respect them and help them. Amen.

AMAZON DEFECTS NOT ALLOWED

> …none of your descendants who has any defect will qualify to offer food to his God.
>
> *- Leviticus 21:17*

Ever ordered something from Amazon or another company online? You can't wait to get it and when you open the package, you hope that it isn't damaged or broken. If it is, you will probably complain and try to figure out how to return it.

God almost seems to be saying the same thing, except this rule applies to people with defects. This seems odd since the Bible says that God loves everyone, but this law also was meant for just priests. At the same time, anyone who had a defect or a handicap was not treated as an outcast. They were not able to perform priestly duties.

Today, this is not the case. Just like in our last devotional, God has made all Christians a part of the priesthood, including people with handicaps. He loves everyone and wants us to participate in the work in a variety of ways.

Talk About It: Do you know a person with a handicap? If so, discuss the variety of ways they can still contribute to the work of God.

Activity: Together, find out if there is someone in your community you could be helping. It might be as small as carrying groceries or maybe someone needs help cutting their lawn.

Prayer: Dear God, thank you for loving everyone and making us all a part of your family. Amen.

The Promise Land

BRAVE SPIES

But Caleb tried to quiet the people as they stood before Moses. "Let's go at once to take the land," he said. "We can certainly conquer it!"

- *Numbers 13:30*

Have you ever had to get ready for a big test? Maybe you were nervous on your first day of school or that interview for the job you wanted. Sometimes we doubt and think of all the things that will go wrong; however, God wants us to be brave.

The Israelites spent 400 years as slaves to the Egyptians and Moses sent twelve spies into the Promises Land. Only two spies came back with a good report, while the other ten said it was impossible. There were giants in the land. Because of their doubts, the ten spies never saw the Promised Land. Instead, the two brave spies were permitted by God and they got to see the impossible become possible.

Talk About It: Have you ever had an impossible moment in your life? Or talk about that big test you ended up passing or maybe the dream job you got that you never thought you would.

Activity: Build a family dream board. Cut out pictures of places you want to go and things you might want to do as a family. Dream a little and think of the many ways you can be brave.

Prayer: Give us great faith and courage just like the two brave spies. Amen.

ROAD TRIP!

Because your men explored the land for forty days, you must wander in the wilderness for forty years

- Numbers 14:34

Some of us get excited about a road trip. Maybe it's to our favourite restaurant or maybe you are going on a big vacation. However, sometimes we get so anxious we begin to wonder if we are ever going to get there.

I'm sure the Israelites were beginning to wonder as they wandered the wilderness for forty years as a punishment for their doubt. There was no sightseeing tour or a stop at a fast food place. It was a constant stop, go, unpack, repack, for forty years.

We also look forward to our destination, but sometimes we miss out on the journey. There might be a lot to see before you get there, so don't be afraid to look out the window and see everything that God has done.

Talk About It - What was the biggest road trip the family has taken? Discuss some of the memories from that trip.

Activity: Plan a road trip to a relative's house or maybe even to a faraway amusement park. Figure out what you are going to do on the journey to keep yourselves occupied.

Prayer: Be with us God as we journey through life and thank you for never leaving us. Amen.

THE GRUMBLING ISRAELITES

Why did you make us leave Egypt and bring us here to this terrible place? This land has no grain, no figs, no grapes, no pomegranates, and no water to drink!

- Numbers 20:5

"I'm hungry!" "I'm thirsty!" "I'm bored!" We sometimes complain a lot, and forget what God has done for us. He has provided for many of us while others will not eat today or have a drink of clean water.

The Israelites started to complain on their road trip and quickly forgot about how the Egyptians used to treat them as slaves. Many of them were beaten for not doing enough work and others had to spend long hours in the sun until their job was done, and yet now they complain about their freedom.

Instead of grumbling about what we don't have, we should take the time to think about the things that make us thankful. To be willing to explore everything that we do have instead of thinking about what we don't have.

Talk About It: Take a moment to discuss other countries in the world that are not as fortunate as we are.

Activity: Decide as a family to help a missionary in another country with at least a one-time offering. You might even want to sponsor a child from another country and then write to that child as a family.

Prayer: Thank you God for giving us everything we have. May we not take it for granted. Amen.

TALKING DONKEYS

Then the Lord gave the donkey the ability to speak.

- Numbers 22:28

I once heard a donkey say, "You might have seen a housefly, maybe even a superfly but I bet you ain't seen a donkey fly." Now, of course, that was in the movie Shrek and not in real life, so we have to remember that in the bible, this donkey talked.

This might seem impossible, however, God is the God of the impossible, plus he had a purpose for it. He was trying to get someone's attention, which I can imagine worked. If I ever heard a donkey talk, it would make me sit up and listen.

Today, God is still trying to get our attention and he is speaking to us through the Bible. Unfortunately, many Bibles sit on bookshelves and they collect dust when they should be read, understood, and followed. So may we sit up, read, and obey.

Talk About It: How is everyone doing with their reading plans? Do we think it is important to read the bible on our own and as a family? Why or why not?

Activity: Do a sword drill. Pick a certain number of bible verses and see who can find them the fastest.

Prayer: We thank you God for giving us the Bible as a way for you to talk to us. Amen.

BE COURAGEOUS

Be strong and courageous, for you are the one who will lead these people to possess all the land I swore to their ancestors I would give them.

- Joshua 1:6

Ever had to do something and yet you had very little experience? It can make a person nervous and scared. The number one fear for people is speaking in public. Most don't want to and yet we see others do so regularly.

God is now appointing Joshua to be the leader and he has some concerns so God tells him to be strong and courageous. He is telling us the same thing, especially when it comes to our faith. We need to be strong and courageous and be willing to tell others how much God loves them.

The good thing is, God is with us every step of the way. We might not be able to see him, but we can be reassured that wherever we go he is telling us to be strong and courageous.

Talk About It: Has anyone been nervous or scared to do something? How did you overcome your fear? Discuss the idea of God being with us.

Activity: Is there someone willing to try and overcome fear? Something like spiders or climbing on a ladder. Suppose you can take some time to help that person overcome their fear and know that God is with you.

Prayer: You have never left us, and you will never forsake us. Thank God, for always being there for us. Amen.

MORE BRAVE SPIES

Then Joshua secretly sent out two spies from the Israelite camp...
- Joshua 2:1

James Bond 007, always seems to be getting into trouble and fighting the bad guys. It is a never-ending movie series where different people throughout the years have played the character and here more spies are being sent out. It's almost like the sequel to a James Bond movie.

Two spies sneaking around and trying not to get caught by the bad guy. In this case, they succeed with the help of a woman named Rahab. They come back and tell the others that they will be able to conquer the land because they have God on their side.

Today, God isn't in the spy business. Instead, he sends out missionaries to tell others about Jesus. This can be just as exciting as being a spy and yet God doesn't just tell the missionaries to do it. He wants all of us to be missionaries wherever we go.

Talk About It: Discuss some of the fears we have when it comes to talking to others about Jesus. How can we overcome them?

Activity: If your church is having an outreach event, sign up as a family and help. If not, maybe try and plan a block party where you can get to know your neighbours.

Prayer: Be with our missionaries and help them do the work you have called them to do. Amen.

Meanwhile, the priests who were carrying the Ark of the Lord's Covenant stood on dry ground in the middle of the riverbed as the people passed by. They waited there until the whole nation of Israel had crossed the Jordan on dry ground.

- Joshua 3:17

Ever heard about a place that is so beautiful and so amazing that you just wanted to see it for yourself? In today's scripture, the people would have heard the story of the first time God parted the water, and now they get to see it.

The priests waited and watched as the people passed by and they saw the waters heaped up on either side. Not only that, but they were on dry ground in the middle of the river. Too bad nobody was taking pictures with their cellphones.

We should marvel at the great things God is still doing today. It might not be as great as parting the river, but he is still performing miracles and we need to be watching for them.

Talk About It: Where have you seen God today or in the past couple of days? What was special about the moment?

Activity: As a family go on a scavenger hunt and take pictures of God's beauty.

Prayer: You are a creative and wonderful God. Thank you for being who you are. Amen.

CRUMBLING BRICKS

When the people heard the sound of the rams' horns, they shouted as loud as they could. Suddenly, the walls of Jericho collapsed, and the Israelites charged straight into the town and captured it.

- Joshua 6:20

God performed some amazing miracles in the Old Testament. We don't often hear about armies walking around a building and then just watching as the bricks come crumbling down by themselves.

However, this reveals how much God loves his children and you are one of his children. He wants to protect you from the bully or others who might want to harm you. But you need to shout as loud as you can and tell others about the people who want to hurt you.

By doing that, your family can help to protect you. There is no need for crumbling bricks when we have the love and support of the people who are closest to us.

Talk About It: Does anyone have a bully or someone who is hurting them? If not, discuss some of the ways that family can help each other against those who would harm us.

Activity: Call a nearby shelter and ask if your family can volunteer for a day. Then go, find out how they protect others and help them.

Prayer: Thank God, for being our protector in times of need. Help us do the same for others. Amen.

AN EXTRA LONG DAY

The sun stayed in the middle of the sky, and it did not set as on a normal day.

- Joshua 10:13

Ever heard of Svalbard? Probably not. It's a place in Norway where the sun doesn't set for about four months of the year. It's known as the land of the midnight sun.

Some of us often think that if we just had a few more hours to the day we could get some more things done, but in Svalbard people still, go to sleep and get up as if it was a regular day. In Joshua's case, he didn't go to sleep. He had the battle to fight, and because the sun didn't set, they won.

However, it shows that God will do what it takes to help us succeed. We may not see extra long days like the people of Svalbard, but when we pray our God is creative and he may cause a different miracle to happen in your life.

Talk About It: Imagine living in Svalbard, Norway. How hard do you think it is to try and sleep when the sun is still shining? Discuss what you might do with the extra amount of sunshine.

Activity: Let's have some fun on a night when nobody has to go to school, work, or church the next day. See who can stay up the longest and decide on a prize for the winner.

Prayer: God, you are our miracle worker. Thank you for doing the impossible. Amen.

BE CAREFUL

So be very careful to follow everything Moses wrote in the Book of Instruction. Do not deviate from it, turning either to the right or to the left.

Sometimes it looks like what our friends are doing is fun. It might be so, but if it goes against the Bible, it usually is only fun for a short time. Then because it was fun we want to do it again and again and it becomes what is called an addiction.

To prevent addiction in our life, we need to be careful in following the Bible. It is a book full of wisdom and insight into life. At times it might be hard to do so, but we have family members and close friends who are willing to help us and encourage us. Stick close to them and be careful.

Talk About It: Here is your chance as a family to talk about addictions. It is never too early. Help everyone to know that they can trust everyone else and that there is help for addictions.

Activity: Call a Christian Rehabilitation Centre near you and see if you and your family can visit and hear about some of the success stories. Suppose you can donate to help them help others.

Prayer: You love us so much that you have provided an instructional manual for life. Thank God for protecting us. Amen.

The Avengers of Israel

OTHNIEL THE DELIVERER

But when the people of Israel cried out to the Lord for help, the Lord raised up a rescuer to save them. His name was Othniel, the son of Caleb's younger brother, Kenaz.

- Judges 3:9

The Avengers, earth's mightiest heroes is a comic book group of superheroes. Of course, they are fictional, but the book of Judges is about earth's mightiest judges who were almost like superheroes in a period between Joshua and the Royal Family.

Othniel the Deliverer is the first and he saved the nation of Israel for the people had begun to go against God. He encouraged everyone to remember everything that God had done for them and as their deliverer, peace in the land of Israel lasted for forty years.

Talk About It: If you were a superhero, what would your superpower be and why?

Activity: Go through the Bible and pick who you think are the superheroes.

Prayer: Thank you God for raising people who help us to stay close to you. Be our guide. Amen.

LEFT-HANDED EHUD

But when the people of Israel cried out to the Lord for help, the Lord again raised up a rescuer to save them. His name was Ehud son of Gera, a left-handed man of the tribe of Benjamin.

- Judges 3:15

Did you know August 13 is the left-handed day? It's a day when we are to celebrate everyone who is left-handed. Now, this doesn't sound like a great superpower but when it comes to baseball, left-handed pitchers have an advantage because most pitchers are right-handed and the batter isn't used to the ball coming from a different angle.

This is what was so great about left-handed Ehud. As an avenger of Israel, the villains did not expect him to attack from the left. This surprise tactical advantage helped him to win his battles and to continue to help Israel succeed.

Talk About It: Is anyone in your family left-handed? Do you know anyone who is left-handed? Discuss whether you think it is harder to live as a left-handed person when most people are right-handed.

Activity: Try to eat with your left hand or write a letter with your left hand. If you are left-handed, try to do these things with your right hand. Discuss how difficult it is.

Prayer: We are all creative differently and with different talents and abilities. Thank you, God. Amen.

SUPER SHAMGAR

After Ehud, Shamgar son of Anath rescued Israel. He once killed 600 Philistines with an ox goad.

- Judges 3:31

Super Shamgar used an ox goad. It's not as powerful as the vibranium shield used by Captain America or Mjolnir the hammer used by Thor. An ox goad is a far cry from any of those. It is a long stick with a pointed end and is sometimes referred to as a cattle prod.

Shamgar was more super than Captain America or Thor because he used a mere stick as his weapon and was able to defeat 600 Philistines. Plus that is all we know about him. This is Shamgar's claim to fame.

Not bad for a day's work, but we must remember that he had God on his side. Unless we are called to defeat 600 Philistines with a stick by God, this activity is highly not recommended. In other words, do not try this at home.

Talk About It: What would you like to be known for? Discuss the importance of leaving a good legacy for yourself.

Activity: Sit down as a family and make an imaginary budget. Have some fun with it. Maybe incorporate a board game like the Game of Life, and demonstrate the importance of working hard.

Prayer: God, you are known for being creative, wonderful, and so much more. Help us to have some of those same qualities so that we can be like you. Make yourself known to others through ourselves. Amen.

PROPHET DEBORAH

Deborah, the wife of Lappidoth, was a prophet who was judging Israel at that time.

- Judges 4:4

Deborah was an exceptional person. Not only was she a woman, and a prophet, but she was also a judge who held court underneath a palm tree. She was wise and helped people solve their problems.

She told the commander of the army of Israel that God wanted him to fight the enemy but he refused to fight unless Prophet Deborah was with him. She went along and helped to defeat the villains. We could almost consider her to be like Captain Marvel but way before her time.

Talk About It: Think about other exceptional women that are godly. What do they do? Why do you consider them to be exceptional? How are they godly? What can we learn from them?

Activity: Send thank you notes to women who have helped the church in some way.

Prayer: Help us God to see how you continue to partner with women in the church. Bless all who serve you. Amen.

GIDEON'S SQUAD

The Lord said to Gideon, "You have too many warriors with you. If I let all of you fight the Midianites, the Israelites will boast to me that they saved themselves by their own strength."

The Avengers had many superheroes to choose from and Gideon had a squad of warriors that were ready to help him at any time. However, one of the most amazing aspects of Gideon is that he was a regular everyday farmer who had doubts.

God called him to defeat the group of people called the Midianites, and he summoned his squad of warriors together. They would win the battle for sure, but God said that was too many. He didn't want anyone to boast and he asked Gideon to send some home.

By the time the fight started, they were outnumbered 50 to 1 and they still won. This revealed that God could use anyone, including an everyday farmer and his squad of ordinary individuals.

Talk About It: Do we ever think we are not good enough? Discuss how God doesn't see us for whom we think we are. Instead, he sees our potential and hopes that we will place our hope in him.

Activity: Come up with a list of five good qualities for everyone in the family.

Prayer: We thank you God for your power in our lives. Help us to trust in you to do great things. Amen.

TOLA THE CRIMSON WORM

After Abimelech died, Tola son of Puah, son of Dodo, was the next person to rescue Israel. He was from the tribe of Issachar but lived in the town of Shamir in the hill country of Ephraim.

- Judges 10:1

Tola, the Crimson Worm, was the son of Dodo, and he was a great rescuer. We don't know much about him, except that he lived in the mountains and during his time there were no villains.

Was he so powerful that everyone was afraid of him? Why is he called the Crimson Worm? In short, the name Tola sometimes means worm, which might seem odd, but names in the bible have special meanings. Therefore, we came up with the Avenger name, The Crimson Worm.

Today, our names still have meanings but we don't always name people according to their characteristics as they did. Sometimes we just name someone because we like the sound of it or it is passed down from another person in the family.

Talk About It: Take a moment to discuss each person's name and why or how they got that name.

Activity: Discover the different meanings of each person's name. Have some fun with it and even look up extended family members.

Prayer: God, you have made each of us unique. Thank you for making us who we are, including our names. Amen.

JAIR AND HIS MANY SONS

His thirty sons rode around on thirty donkeys, and they owned thirty towns in the land of Gilead, which are still called the Towns of Jair.

- Judges 10:4

Jair didn't have any superhuman strength, nor was he able to fly. Instead, he had thirty sons and together they owned thirty towns. They also didn't need any superpowers because they had no villains to fight.

However, with nobody to worry about, the people of Israel got bored and they began to ignore God. They looked toward the false gods of other nations and caused their problems amongst themselves.

Isn't it sad, how we cry out to God when we need him the most, but when things are good, we tend to ignore him? We hope that isn't the case with you and we hope your family seeks God every day.

Talk About It: What false gods can we have today? Discuss what can lead us away from God.

Activity: Find ways to strengthen your relationship with God.

Prayer: Help us God to always love you with our whole hearts, mind, strength, and soul. May we never forget you. Amen.

JEPHTHAH, THE PROMISE BREAKER

I will give to the Lord whatever comes out of my house to meet me when I return in triumph. I will sacrifice it as a burnt offering.

- Judges 11:31

Jephthah is one of the great Avengers of Israel. He even made it to the Hall of Faith and yet he broke a promise. He promised that whatever came out of his house first, he would sacrifice in a burnt offering. Unfortunately, his daughter was the first.

This seems like a good promise to break and reminds us that we should be careful about what we promise. God doesn't want us to go back on what we say. We should let our yes be yes and our no be no, and yet Jephthah makes the Hall of Faith and the Holy Spirit still came upon him. It is an amazing example of God's love and forgiveness.

Talk About It: We have all done wrong. Discuss how hard it is to forgive someone for breaking a promise. Should God have forgiven Jephthan and why?

Activity: Take time as a family to make a meal together. Give each person a role to play and learn the importance of working together and how valuable each person in the family is.

Prayer: Thank you to everyone in our family. Help us not to take each other for granted and learn to love one another. Amen.

IBZAN THE FATHER OF COLDNESS

He had thirty sons and thirty daughters. He sent his daughters to marry men outside his clan, and he brought in thirty young women from outside his clan to marry his sons. Ibzan judged Israel for seven years.

- Judges 12:9

Ibzan is the Father of Coldness because he is known for sending away his thirty daughters and bringing thirty young women from another country to marry his sons. This means that sixty women had to move to strange new places and be with people they didn't know.

This might seem strange, but during biblical times, you didn't have a choice of whom to marry. Your parents made a choice. Sometimes the person would be near you, but other times you might have to move far away. However, for Ibzan this is a little strange.

Today, we can be thankful that we get to make our own choice. However, God wants us to choose wisely because marriage is a decision we are supposed to make for life.

Talk About It: Parents, discuss some of the difficulties of marriage.

Activity: It's Parent Appreciation time! Do something special for your parents.

Prayer: God, we thank you for our parents. Please give them to strength to continue to provide a safe and loving home. Amen.

ELON THE ZEBULUNITE

After Ibzan died, Elon from the tribe of Zebulun judged Israel for ten years.

- Judges 12:11

Today, we look at Elon. Not Elon Musk! Elon the Zebulunite. Now, compared to Elon Musk, this Elon doesn't seem important. There is no mention of a battle and all we know is that he comes from the tribe of Zebulun and he served for ten years.

Even ten years is a short time in comparison to some of our other avengers. But what we do know is that Elon took over from Ibzan and that is important.

Have you ever watched the Olympics and how people pass the flame from one person to another? Elon is important because he carried on the work and eventually he passed it to another person. It might be nice to be known for your billions of dollars but sometimes it is better to be known for just doing a good job.

Talk About It: Have you ever done something and nobody noticed it? How did it make you feel? Why?

Activity: Do something nice for someone else in the family but don't let them know you did it. See if others can guess who did what.

Prayer: Help us God to be people who help others without asking for anything in return. Amen.

SERVANT ABDON

He had forty sons and thirty grandsons, who rode on seventy donkeys. He judged Israel for eight years.

- Judges 12:14

Abdon is another one of these avengers we know very little about. His name means servant and he was best known for having forty sons and thirty grandsons. Now that's a lot!

For some reason, they also didn't ride on horses. Instead, they decided they liked to ride on donkeys. Hee-Haw! Could you just imagine the noise of seventy donkeys all at once? Not only that, but donkeys can be stubborn and they don't always do what they are told.

Plus donkeys were a sign of service. It seems Abdon didn't want to be known as an Avenger. Instead, he wanted to be best known as a person who served others. How amazing is that?

Talk About It: Discuss Abdon, a person of wealth, who owned lots of donkeys, and compare him to other people of wealth. Do you find Abdon to be amazing and why?

Activity: If you could be a millionaire, what would you do with the money and why? Take some time to think about it. Come up with plans as individuals and then come back together and discuss your plans.

Prayer: Lord, make us be servants. People who will honour you in all that we do. Amen.

STRONGMAN SAMSON

At that moment the Spirit of the Lord came powerfully upon him, and he ripped the lion's jaws apart with his bare hands. He did it as easily as if it were a young goat. But he didn't tell his father or mother about it.

Unlike the last few avengers of judges of the Bible, we know a lot about Samson. Most of it isn't good. He made quite a few mistakes and it usually had to do with the influence of women upon his life.

That didn't stop God from being a part of his life. The Holy Spirit still worked through him in powerful ways and he was able to rip a lion's jaw with his bare hands. At the end of his life, he destroyed a whole temple to defeat the villains who had captured him.

This isn't an excuse to help us do wrong, but it is a good reminder that God will overlook our mistakes to be a part of our lives. Therefore, may be thankful that God is willing to partner with us to help others.

Talk About It: Is there something you don't feel confident in? How can God help you? Discuss some ways that God can help us to overcome our mistakes.

Activity: Did someone in the family make a mistake or do they have fear? Find a way to help them overcome that mistake or fear.

Prayer: Thank God for helping us overcome our mistakes and fears. Amen.

Women Of The Bible

RUTH THE MOABITE

Wherever you go, I will go; wherever you live, I will live. Your people will be my people, and your God will be my God.

- Ruth 1:16

Women are important in the Bible and one of the most faithful of all women was Ruth. She lost everything, including her husband and she decided that she wanted to stick around and help her mother-in-law.

God rewarded her by helping her to find another husband and later they would be blessed with a son. That son was the grandfather of King David who was an ancestor to Jesus. But none of that would have happened if Ruth didn't decide to stay with her mother-in-law.

Taking care of family is important and God honours that. Hopefully, God will bless you with the privilege of being able to take care of some of your elderly relatives. We know you will be blessed because of it.

Talk About It: Discuss some of the pros and cons of taking care of our elderly relatives.

Activity: If possible, it's time to visit Grandma and Grandpa. Take time to learn about your family history. If you are not able to, visit an elderly person in your church.

Prayer: Thank you for blessing us with people whom we can learn from. May you help us to surround them with your love. Amen.

EVE

Then the man—Adam—named his wife Eve, because she would be the mother of all who live.

- Genesis 3:20

Eve was the first woman and she is the mother of everyone. She also saw God face to face and lived in the Garden of Eden. This was an amazing time to be alive.

Imagine living in a beautiful garden where all the animals got along and you were able to walk with God in the cool of the day. It is hard to believe that both Eve and her husband, Adam, gave all of that up for a piece of fruit.

Unfortunately, we sometimes make the same mistake. It might just be a candy bar in a store or some coins left on the table. We still feel tempted and we take it. Hopefully, we can learn from both Eve and our own mistakes.

Talk About It: What is the smallest and silliest mistake you ever made? Why did you do it? What did you learn?

Activity: Take a trip to a garden or a park and admire all the beauty. Make a note of the different animals and colours. Then give thanks to God for all he has created.

Prayer: May we always learn to appreciate everything you do for us, God. Let us not take you for granted. Amen.

SARAH

God replied, "No—Sarah, your wife, will give birth to a son for you. You will name him Isaac, and I will confirm my covenant with him and his descendants as an everlasting covenant.

- Genesis 17:19

Can you imagine having a baby at the age of 90?! Sarah not only couldn't believe it, but she also laughed at the idea. I'm pretty sure I would laugh also. It is an impossible situation and yet God chooses this wonderful woman to perform an amazing miracle.

Maybe today you are praying for a miracle but when you think about it, you almost want to laugh at the idea of it ever coming true. Our God is the God of the impossible and we should never give up. For at just the right time, he will perform the miracle that you will need.

Talk About It: Has God ever performed a miracle within the family? Take the time to discuss it or maybe talk about the miracles you want God to do.

Activity: Make a prayer list for the family and begin to pray about each situation. Mark down the date you began to pray and then when the prayer is answered, mark the date and give thanks to God.

Prayer: We surrender our problems to you God and we ask that you would perform a miracle in our lives. Amen.

RACHEL

Then God remembered Rachel's plight and answered her prayers by enabling her to have children.

- Genesis 30:22

Sometimes we want to give our children everything that they ever wanted. The same goes for our spouse and other people that we love. Rachel was no different, except that she couldn't give her husband any children.

She wondered what was wrong with her. The Bible doesn't even really give us any explanation and even tells us that her husband loved her the most. However, for years she struggled and could not give her husband a child.

After many years of praying, she eventually gave birth to a son and then later was able to have a second son. God remembered her and never forgot her. He doesn't forget you either. Even though your prayer has not been answered, you are not forgotten.

Talk About It: Does it ever feel like God has forgotten us? Why do we think that why? How can we remember that he will never leave us or forsake us?

Activity: Find a local museum of history and take the time to learn or remember some local history that has been forgotten.

Prayer: We know that you have never forgotten us. Thank you, God, for always being there for us. Amen.

MIRIAM

And Miriam sang this song: "Sing to the Lord, for he has triumphed gloriously; he has hurled both horse and rider into the sea."

- Exodus 15:21

Sometimes we spend more time fighting with our brother or sister than we do helping. Maybe we want to punch them for taking our toy or wearing our clothes and guess what? Miriam is the sister of Moses. Ever wonder if she wanted to punch Moses?

Well, the Bible tells us that it was Miriam who helped Moses be reconnected to his mother as a baby. It was also Miriam who helped Moses to lead the nation of Israel along with their brother Aaron. She was a woman of great courage and she was a good sibling.

We can learn a lot from Miriam. Hopefully, today, you can learn ways to help your brother or sister. If you don't have any, it will be a good chance to help a friend or your parents.

Talk About It: Discuss a time when someone in the family fought with a brother or sister. How did you reconcile? Was it easy?

Activity: Road trip to an Uncle or an Aunt's house. Learn more about them and how they grew up.

Prayer: Thank you God for giving us brothers and sisters, along with friends and parents. Help us to always be nice to them. Amen.

Those who fight against the Lord will be shattered. He thunders against them from heaven; the Lord judges throughout the earth. He gives power to his king; he increases the strength of his anointed one.

- 1 Samuel 2:10

Have you ever met a prayer warrior? Someone who spends a lot of time talking to God. You may think it is your pastor or someone else in the church. Maybe you are blessed enough to have a prayer warrior in the family.

Hannah is a prayer warrior and she gives all she has to tell God that she wants a son. She even goes as far as to tell God that she will give him her son back. Hannah also follows through with her promise because she knows that we all belong to God.

The people in our family all belong to God and we are all his children. This makes part of an even bigger and more special family. They may not all live in the house with you, but if they believe in God and they believe in Jesus, then they are also your brother and sister.

Talk About It: Take a moment to discuss the idea of God's family and the church. If your church performs dedication ceremonies, now is a good time to talk about the significance.

Activity: Visit close friends in the church or invite some people over for dinner and give thanks to the brothers and sisters God gives to us.

Prayer: We give thanks for the church and we give thanks for the wonderful people you put in our lives. Amen.

QUEEN ESTHER

Who knows if perhaps you were made queen for just such a time as this?

- Esther 4:14

Queen Esther was crowned at just the right time. Many people were against the Jews and the King ordered a decree that on a certain day people were allowed to attack and kill anyone who was a Jew. However, the King did not know that his own Queen was also a Jew.

Esther managed to convince the King to change his law, for it could not be undone. This allowed the Jews to at least defend themselves if they were attacked. Therefore, when the day arrived, nothing happened.

She was appointed queen to save the Jews, and you have been appointed disciples of Jesus to help save people who don't know Christ. Just like Queen Esther, you were born for just such a time as this.

Talk About It: Discuss why we need to help save people who don't know Christ and what we can do as disciples.

Activity: As a family, make a list of friends or family members who don't know Christ. Begin to pray for them and ask God to help you make disciples.

Prayer: We praise you God for creating us at such a time as this. Help us to be able to help others. Amen.

MARY MAGDALENE

Early on Sunday morning, as the new day was dawning, Mary Magdalene and the other Mary went out to visit the tomb.

- Matthew 28:1

Mary Magdalene was a disciple of Jesus. She had been possessed by demons and it was Jesus who cast the demons away. For that, she was grateful and followed him everywhere he went. We even discover that she was there when Jesus died on the cross.

It should be no surprise to us that Mary is one of the women who went to the tomb to visit the body of Jesus. However, when they got there, they discovered that the tomb was empty. Jesus had risen from the dead.

Can you imagine how much joy she would have felt? Someone she deeply admired was no longer dead, and everything he had said must be true. Jesus did die and rise again for the forgiveness of our sins.

Talk About It: What does it mean to us that Jesus died and rose again? How has this made a difference in our lives?

Activity: Mary was thankful for what Jesus had done. Is there someone or a group of people you are thankful for? Write a thank you card to the police station, medical clinic, school, or an individual.

Prayer: Thank you God for how you have changed our lives. Help us to be as grateful as Mary Magdalene. Amen.

"Don't be afraid, Mary," the angel told her, "for you have found favour with God!"

- Luke 1:30

Have you ever wanted to be the most popular kid in school? Maybe you hoped to be the one your boss approves of at work. To be liked or to be approved of by someone means that you have found favour. Mary wasn't the most popular kid, nor did she have a boss that approved of her. Instead, she found favour with God!

How amazing is that?! She was given the privilege of being the mother of Jesus. This is how much favour she had with God. It's almost like she is God's favourite, but the Bible also tells us that he has no favourites. This means you can also find favour with God.

You won't give birth to someone like Jesus. That job was already taken. However, God has a different job for you and because you are favoured, he desires that you discover what it is and walk with him to accomplish all he has for you.

Talk About It: Do you feel like you are favoured by God? Why or why not?

Activity: Take time this week to discover everything you can do for God. As a family come back together and pick one thing out of everyone's list and do it.

Prayer: Help us to know how much you truly favour us. Thank you for always being with us. Amen.

ELIZABETH

At the sound of Mary's greeting, Elizabeth's child leaped within her, and Elizabeth was filled with the Holy Spirit.

- Luke 1:41

There are moments in our life when we get to celebrate the birth of a new baby. Today, we even have gender reveal parties and baby showers before the big day. Designing the baby's new room and making sure everything is just right when the moment arrives.

When Mary was pregnant she went to go see her cousin Elizabeth who was also pregnant and the baby inside of Elizabeth began to celebrate for the baby inside of Mary was Jesus. That seems like a greater celebration than anything we can do.

We should always look for the great moments in everyone's life. Especially the day when they come to know Jesus as their Saviour. This should be a moment marked on people's calendars and celebrated just like a birthday.

Talk About It: Does everyone know what it means to be born again? What happened on that special day when you gave your life to Christ? Share your stories.

Activity: Begin to mark on your calendars, the day of your second birth. Celebrate these days in your unique way.

Prayer: Thank you God for second chances. Help us to celebrate and rejoice in all you have done for us. Amen.

MARY, SISTER OF MARTHA

There is only one thing worth being concerned about. Mary has discovered it, and it will not be taken away from her.

- Luke 10:42

Do you ever feel like you are doing more chores than everyone else in the house? Did you get upset because others seem lazy? What did you do about it? Martha got upset with her sister Mary and complained to Jesus.

Mary was sitting at the feet of Jesus and listening while Martha was trying to make everything perfect for their guests. Jesus listened to her concern and told Martha that Mary was doing what was important.

Sometimes we can get so concerned with how clean the house is or how things look to others. Jesus, however, wants us to be more concerned about our relationship with him. Right now, you are doing what you should be doing. Growing closer together as a family and growing closer to God. Keep it up and don't let away take it away from you.

Talk About It: Review how your family devotions have been going. What have you liked about it?

Activity: You have done many things as a family so far. Pick your favourite and redo it. Relive some of those memories.

Prayer: Continue to help us come closer as a family. Thank you for each one and the role they play and thank you God for being in the centre of it. Amen.

PRISCILLA

When Priscilla and Aquila heard him preaching boldly in the synagogue, they took him aside and explained the way of God even more accurately.

- Acts 18:26

One church has recently celebrated its first woman in a leadership role. Other churches don't believe this should be possible, while many more have female pastors and have no problems with female leaders. Depending on your beliefs you may have had a hard time with this section or you might be shouting, "Amen" all the way.

Priscilla is often listed before her husband because she is the most involved in the church. Her husband was the helpmate and together the two of them took a person aside and explained who God was more accurately.

God has made us co-heirs in Christ. He has given a job to both men and women and it is up to us to search our hearts to discover what that job is. As a family, it is up to you to figure out how you will work together to accomplish his task for you.

Talk About It: How do you feel about women leaders/pastors in the church? Have the last few devotionals changed minds?

Activity: Find a female pastor. Set up a time to meet with her and ask her about the struggles she has had to go through.

Prayer: Thank you God for giving godly female role models for us to follow. Help us to know our roles as co-heirs in Christ. Amen.

The Royal Family

THE FIRST KING

"Do everything they say to you," the Lord replied, "for they are rejecting me, not you. They don't want me to be their king any longer.

- 1 Samuel 8:7

After the Avengers of Israel, better known as Judges, the nation of Israel began to cry out for a king. All the other nations that surrounded them had kings and they wanted the same. How quickly they had forgotten. They already had a king and he was God.

He is the King of kings and the Lord of lords, but God gave into the needs of his people and gave them what they wanted. A king. His name was Saul and he was tall, handsome, and good. Unfortunately, this did not last.

Eventually, the power given to Saul turned him into a bad person and he was not a good king. Revealing to us that not everyone can handle the position and we should always be careful to whom we give power.

Talk About It: Discuss some of the great leaders and what makes them great.

Activity: Have some fun and do an election of who will be president of the family. List some campaign promises and see who is the most promising.

Prayer: God, you are the King of kings and the Lord of lords. Help us never to forget that. Amen.

But the Lord said to Samuel, "Don't judge by his appearance or height, for I have rejected him. The Lord doesn't see things the way you see them. People judge by outward appearance, but the Lord looks at the heart."

- 1 Samuel 16:7

Ever pick teams in the schoolyard? Have you ever been picked last? If not, think about the kid who was picked last. Why was that person last? Probably because they were not the strongest or the fastest.

When it came time to pick King Saul's replacement, Samuel the prophet went to a family who had eight sons. The father called in seven of his sons and left the youngest out in the field. He wasn't the best out of them all, yet the Bible still says he had a fine appearance and handsome features.

God picked the youngest. Not for his strength or his appearance. He saw his heart and who he would become. That day, David was anointed as the next king.

Talk About It: Do you ever feel like you are not good enough? Why? What can help us to overcome it? Discuss how God sees us.

Activity: Write good features of every person in your family. Encourage each other and help to reveal how God sees everyone.

Prayer: Help us God to see ourselves how you see us. You see what is on the inside. Thank you. Amen.

GOLIATH

Reaching into his shepherd's bag and taking out a stone, he hurled it with his sling and hit the Philistine in the forehead. The stone sank in, and Goliath stumbled and fell face down on the ground.

- 1 Samuel 17:49

David was anointed king, but he didn't become king right away. He had to wait, and while he was waiting, he had this amazing moment where he stood up against a giant. The army of Israel was all afraid of him, but David knew that God was with him.

Without any armour and only a slingshot and five stones, he went out into the middle of the field to face the giant. The giant laughed at such a small person. This did not stop him. He grabbed the first stone, put it in the slingshot and fired.

The stone hit the giant in the forehead and he fell. David ran towards the giant, grabbed the giant's sword, and cut his head off. David won because God was with him.

Talk About It: God doesn't call us to fight giants, but there are times when we face big problems. Discuss some of those big problems and how we can fight them with God's help.

Activity: Ever watched the movie, Facing the Giants? It's a Christian drama sports movie about a football team. Have a movie night as a family and maybe rewatch the movie.

Prayer: Thank you God for helping us to face our giants. Amen.

TRUE FRIENDSHIP

After David had finished talking with Saul, he met Jonathan, the king's son. There was an immediate bond between them, for Jonathan loved David.

- 1 Samuel 18:1

Ever have a best friend? Someone you like to hang out with. Maybe you spend most of your free time with this person or play a lot of sports with them. God gives us friends.

David's best friend was Jonathon, King Saul's son. They immediately liked each other and wanted to hang out. The bible even says that Jonathan loved David, but of course, this isn't the same love between a husband and a wife.

Love is an interesting word. We can love pizza but we can also love our friends. We might not say it the same way; however, when we are close to a friend, we will do almost anything for them. That is love in the form of a friendship.

Talk About It: Take the word love and talk about the different ways you can love.

Activity: Each person in the family can invite one of their friends over and have an appreciation night for your friends.

Prayer: Thank you God for giving us, friends. Amen.

SECOND CHANCES

May the Lord reward you well for the kindness you have shown me today.

- 1 Samuel 24:19

Did someone ever hurt you and you wanted to get back at them? Maybe they even punched you first and you wanted to punch back. Sometimes when a person gets cut off in traffic the driver wants to speed up and do the same for the other person.

King Saul was jealous that David was going to be the next king instead of his son. He wanted to kill David and so David ran away. Saul chased him and while David was in hiding he had the opportunity to kill Saul, but he didn't. When Saul discovered this, that is when he said, "May the Lord reward you well for the kindness you have shown me today."

He saw the heart of David and was thankful that he didn't want to kill him even though he wanted to kill David. Sometimes, we need to be bigger and show kindness instead of anger.

Talk About It: Was there a moment when you wanted to get revenge? How can we overcome these moments?

Activity: Discuss a way you can be kind to your neighbours and then pick one of them and do it.

Prayer: Help us Lord to always show kindness. Allow us to be your light in the neighbourhood. Amen.

So David reigned over all Israel and did what was just and right for all his people.

- 2 Samuel 8:15

Did the family ever plan a trip and it seemed to take forever before we could go? The excitement just kept building and even on the night before you were to go, you couldn't sleep. You just wanted the moment to finally happen.

David felt the same way. He was anointed king at a young age and had to wait until he could feel the crown on top of his head. He went through many struggles along the way and it didn't seem like the day was ever going to happen. Finally, the day came.

How great that must have felt. All of the emotions didn't ruin the moment because the Bible says that he did what was just and right for everyone. We should make the most of our best moments and do all we can to make sure they are good.

Talk About It: Discuss some of the best moments of your life that you had to wait for. Was it worth it? Would you do anything differently?

Activity: If you can plan to go somewhere fun but take some time to save and make sure that whatever you are going to do will be fun for the whole family.

Prayer: God, you give us good things and sometimes we have to wait for them. Thank you for providing it at just the right time. Amen.

SHOW KINDNESS

One day David asked, "Is anyone in Saul's family still alive—anyone to whom I can show kindness for Jonathan's sake?"

- 2 Samuel 9:1

Ever receive a homemade baked pie from the next-door neighbour or someone in your church? Maybe it was given because someone in the family had passed away. It feels good to have been shown kindness by someone else.

David wanted to show kindness to someone who was related to his best friend Jonathon. Jonathon was now gone and David was now distant from the family, but he found Jonathan's son who was crippled. David essentially adopted this young man and made him a part of his family.

This type of kindness is extreme, but we can learn a lesson about how to treat others. To go the extra distance to make sure someone knows how much you truly care about them.

Talk About It: Think of a time when you were shown kindness or you showed kindness to someone else. How did that make you feel? Discuss the importance of showing kindness.

Activity: Show kindness to your neighbours. Bake a pie, cut the grass, or shovel some snow.

Prayer: God, you are the one that has shown the most kindness to all. Thank you. Amen.

DELIGHT IN THE LAW

But they delight in the law of the Lord, meditating on it day and night.

- Psalm 1:2

King David also wrote many of the Psalms. He was a musician who delighted in the law for it was what kept many people focused on pleasing God. Today, Jesus fulfilled that law, but it doesn't mean we ignore it.

Just like when we come up to a stop sign, we stop and look both ways because there might be cars coming the other way. If we ignore this, people can get hurt or even worse; they might die.

This is why God made the law. It is for our protection. He doesn't want any of us to get hurt and David is delighted in the law. He sang about it and meditated upon it. We should learn of ways to do the same in our life.

Talk About It: How do you feel about the law? Is it too restrictive or do you appreciate it? How can the law be beneficial?

Activity: Have some fun. Look up and find weird and funny laws in your country.

Prayer: Thank you God for your law that is perfect and good. Help us to think upon it and obey it. Amen.

But God removed Saul and replaced him with David, a man about whom God said, 'I have found David son of Jesse, a man after my own heart. He will do everything I want him to do.'

- Acts 13:22

Ever heard of Michael Jordan? If not, you may have heard of Air Jordans, the running shoes. They were named after him and his love for sports. He loved sports so much that when he didn't make the basketball team in high school, he didn't let that stop him.

According to the official NBA website, Jordan is "the greatest basketball player of all time." It is because he chased after his passion, and King David was known as a man after God's own heart. He chased after his passion for God.

Both Jordan and David made mistakes along the way, but they are both known for what and who they loved the most. Through this, we can learn about who we are and what we are most passionate about.

Talk About It: What are your passions? What do you want to be known for and how do you plan to pursue your dreams?

Activity: What do you want your family to be known for? Develop a vision chart for your family and come up with ways to achieve your goals.

Prayer: Help us God to be known as people who chase after your heart. May we be more like you. Amen.

THE WISEST KING?

God gave Solomon very great wisdom and understanding, and knowledge as vast as the sands of the seashore.

- 1 Kings 4:29

King Solomon was the last king under a united nation. After him, Israel became divided. However, Solomon was also known as the wisest because God gave Solomon what he asked for. He didn't want to be richer, nor did he want more land. Instead, Solomon wanted to be wise.

However, Solomon had 700 wives. It doesn't seem like the wisest decision he has ever made. It distracted him from being able to worship God and today, and God doesn't want us to be distracted from him.

We can so easily lose sight of God in our lives. It might be as small as a toy or as we get older it might be another person. Solomon just proves to us that we can be the wisest person in the world and still allow distractions to push us further from God.

Talk About It: Discuss some of the distractions in life. What can we do to prevent these distractions from ruining our relationship with God?

Activity: As a family go for a walk to a park or on a nature trail. Give everyone a short verse to repeat over and over in your mind. As everyone silently walks notice how quickly you become distracted from repeating the verse.

Prayer: May we focus on you, God. To know you is best. Amen.

Prophets

ELIJAH ON MOUNT CARMEL

Immediately the fire of the Lord flashed down from heaven and burned up the young bull, the wood, the stones, and the dust. It even licked up all the water in the trench!

- 1 Kings 18:38

Ever watched lighting come from the sky? Maybe you have been given a chance to see it roll off the roof of a house. However, I don't imagine you have ever seen fire flash down from heaven unless it was in a movie.

Not only did this happen, but it happened at a time when the land was going without water. Elijah managed to find water, pour it on the altar and prove to everyone watching that the God he served was the real deal.

Everyone was amazed and Elijah showed that he was a man of great faith. Today, God is looking for people just like Elijah. Men, women, boys and girls who will stand up for him.

Talk About It: What are some ways that you can stand up for God? In school? At work? Even in your neighbourhood?

Activity: Read 1 Kings 18:1-40 and maybe try to act it out and have some fun with it.

Prayer: Thank you for the great men and women of faith. Help us God to be more like them. Amen.

GOD'S CALLING

So Elijah went and found Elisha son of Shaphat plowing a field. There were twelve teams of oxen in the field, and Elisha was plowing with the twelfth team. Elijah went over to him and threw his cloak across his shoulders and then walked away.

- 1 Kings 19:19

Did you know you have a calling in your life? Sometimes we think of the pastor or the other paid people at the church as the ones who call has called. He has called them, but he also calls you. Our pastors, teachers, and evangelists need you to be a part of the team.

Notice Elisha was working in the field when he was called. He was an ordinary human being. The people you see on stage every Sunday morning are also ordinary human beings. Sometimes the only difference is, they are living out their calling, while others have yet to discover it.

Many people will never get a moment like Elisha, while others will. However, what we need to realize the most is that we are all on God's team and we all have a calling in our lives. We just need to discover and walk in it.

Talk About It: Do you feel like you have a calling in your life? What is it? What can the family do to help you in that calling? If you don't, how can we discover it?

Activity: Make an appointment with a pastor at your church. Ask about his or her calling and how they knew.

Prayer: We thank you God for making us a part of your team. Help us to do our part. Amen.

CHARIOT OF FIRE

As they were walking along and talking, suddenly a chariot of fire appeared, drawn by horses of fire. It drove between the two men, separating them, and Elijah was carried by a whirlwind into heaven.

- 2 Kings 2:11

Everything eventually has to be passed on. In a relay race, runners pass a baton so that the next person can carry on the race until the last one crosses the finish line. Nobody can say that they did it on their own. It takes a whole team to complete the job.

It came time for Elijah to go to heaven dramatically and beautifully, but there was still work to be done. It was now Elisha's turn to carry on the work. The baton was being passed on and it would be up to Elisha to finish the race.

The baton is still being passed and it has now been passed to you. As you hold it in your hand, know that it is an honour to be chosen. Run your race well.

Talk About It: What are our responsibilities as believers? As a family discuss what we can be doing to help everyone run their race well.

Activity: Set up an obstacle course in the backyard. If there are enough members of the family split them into two teams. If not, invite another family over and have a competition. Learn how to work together to win.

Prayer: As a family, help us to work together. Build us up so that we can run our race well. Amen.

BULLIES

Elisha left Jericho and went up to Bethel. As he was walking along the road, a group of boys from the town began mocking and making fun of him. "Go away, baldy!" they chanted. "Go away, baldy!"

- 2 Kings 3:23

Ever heard the saying, "Sticks and stones may break my bones, but names will never hurt me." It isn't true. Names do hurt and bullies come in all shapes and sizes. Plus it used to be something that only happened at school or work, but today we have cyberbullies and it is becoming a bigger problem.

Elisha was made fun of and the bible says that he cursed them. After that two bears came out and mauled the bullies. Now that seems like a cool thing to happen and it almost seems like God asked the two bears to do it. However, the bible doesn't say God did it.

We should also not want revenge on our bullies. Instead, we should talk about it and seek help from others. It might be a parent, a principal, or a boss. If the situation gets out of hand, you might need the help of the police, but we should never try to defeat a bully on our own.

Talk About It: Does anyone have any bullies? Discuss it and look at ways of helping one another.

Activity: Take the time to learn about support hotlines in your area and what resources your family could use now or possibly in the future.

Prayer: Protect us God and help us against bullies. Amen.

NO FOOD

One day the widow of a member of the group of prophets came to Elisha and cried out, "My husband who served you is dead, and you know how he feared the Lord. But now a creditor has come, threatening to take my two sons as slaves."

- 2 Kings 4:1

Sometimes families have a hard time making ends meet. Decisions have to be made between paying a certain bill or buying food from the store. We can be thankful that nobody is going door to door collecting children to pay our debts.

The widow was not so fortunate, but God took care of her. He filled her jars with olive oil and she was able to sell the oil at the market and make enough money to pay off her debts. She was able to keep her two sons.

Today, many organizations help families to get food. Your church might even be one of them. Overall, we can be thankful for everything that God has provided us.

Talk About It: Discuss some of the meals you have had recently. Imagine going without food. How do you think that would make you feel?

Activity: If you can, participate in a fast or join a fundraiser that helps to teach about hunger in your own country or another country.

Prayer: Thank you God for the food you provide for us. Help us to help others. Amen.

NAAMAN THE LEPER

So Naaman went down to the Jordan River and dipped himself seven times, as the man of God had instructed him. And his skin became as healthy as the skin of a young child, and he was healed!

- 2 Kings 5:14

Naaman was a leper. This isn't short for leopard. I don't mean a large cat with black spots that makes a growling noise when it's mad or hungry. Naaman had a disease called leprosy and in biblical times it would cause a variety of marks on your skin.

Nobody could go near you for it was against the law and you might also become a leper. For the most part, it was unknown and there was no cure. You could only pray to God and hope that he might heal you.

We also have many diseases that we have no cure. There are times in our life when all we can do is pray. In Naaman's case, he was healed. Many others have had the same experience and God still heals today.

Talk About It: When should we go to the hospital? Are there times we should stay home and pray? Discuss as a family your beliefs on how God heals.

Activity: Find out if you can help your pastor do a hospital visit. Discover what is involved in visitation.

Prayer: Be with us God and keep us healthy. Amen.

PROPHETS TELL ABOUT JESUS

In that day Judah will be saved, and Jerusalem will live in safety. And this will be its name: 'The Lord Is Our Righteousness.'

- Jeremiah 33:16

Have you ever gone somewhere and when you walked in the house, the host apologized for the mess? Looking around, everything seems tidy, but in their mind, it's not perfect. They see something is out of place and sometimes they are even embarrassed.

Well God was doing that with the prophets. As they talked about Jesus, many prophets were trying to prepare the people for his arrival. This was such an important event, and God spent centuries getting ready. He wanted everything to be just right.

The prophets also talk about how Jesus will come back. God is again preparing and he wants everything to be just right for when he returns. For now, we can be thankful that he came the first time and take the time to learn more about him.

Talk About It: How do we know Jesus will return? How can we be ready?

Activity: Have some fun. Pick a sports game and predict who will win. Sit down as the family and watch the game and find out who is right.

Prayer: Thank you for your son Jesus and thank you that he will return. Amen.

Jesus

JESUS IS BORN

The Saviour—yes, the Messiah, the Lord—has been born today in Bethlehem, the city of David!

- Luke 2:11

It might not be Christmas yet, but every year we celebrate Christmas as the day when Jesus was born. For some families, this is a big event and depending upon where you live there could be great anticipation for the day to finally arrive. The presents under the tree and the big family meal that everyone will enjoy.

Before Jesus was born, many couldn't wait for the day to arrive. The only problem was, they didn't know when he was going to be born. There was no day called Christmas yet and it wasn't about presents or family meals. Instead, they wanted to be saved.

That was Jesus' purpose. He is our Saviour and if we believe in him, he will save us from everything we have done wrong so that we can one day go to heaven.

Talk About It: Imagine what your life would be without Jesus. Discuss how important he is to us.

Activity: Don't wait for Christmas. Pick a day and celebrate it with a birthday cake for Jesus instead of presents and a big meal.

Prayer: We thank you God for giving us a Saviour. Amen.

STORMS

When Jesus woke up, he rebuked the wind and said to the waves, "Silence! Be still!" Suddenly the wind stopped, and there was a great calm.

- Mark 4:39

There are days when the sky goes all dark, the winds pick up and it looks like the trees are going to come out of the ground. We probably all have gone through some pretty bad storms and sometimes in our lives, it feels like everything is going wrong. We call them storms also.

The great thing about Jesus is that he could stop any kind of storm. He told the wind to stop and it did. Soon the waves stopped and the lake they were in was calm. There are also times in our life when we pray that God would calm other types of storms. That he would make our bad days into good.

Amazingly enough, he can. We just need to learn to focus on him and trust him. He cares enough for us to turn our bad days into good.

Talk About It: Remember a time when God turned a bad day into a good one. Share the story with the rest of the family so everyone can be encouraged.

Activity: Help give someone else a good day. Children may surprise their parents by making them breakfast. Parents, surprise your kids with something. Mom and dad, surprise each other.

Prayer: Turn our bad days into good. Help us to trust you, God. Amen.

THIRSTY?

But those who drink the water I give will never be thirsty again. It becomes a fresh, bubbling spring within them, giving them eternal life.

- John 4:14

Ever felt your mouth go dry? All of a sudden you have a craving for a drink of water, juice, or something else. You just can't wait to have that drink. To taste it and to feel refreshed.

Jesus is talking about something similar. He is offering us a different kind of water. It isn't what we get from a tap or a bottle. Instead, this water type of water only comes from him and it refreshes our soul, not our body.

The only way we can drink this water is if we ask Jesus to be our Saviour. The moment we do that, our soul, the spiritual part within us, drinks this water and we are given the gift of eternal life.

Talk About It: Discuss the gift of eternal life and how our soul is given eternal life.

Activity: If anyone just asked for Jesus to be their Saviour, plan to have a baptism or a celebration. It is a great moment and there needs to be a party.

Prayer: Thank you God for the water that gives us the gift of eternal life. Amen.

WALKING ON WATER

About three o'clock in the morning Jesus came toward them, walking on the water.

- Matthew 14:25

Have you ever tried to walk on water? Maybe even get a running start and only find out every time you sink. Now, this might sound silly to you and so you have never even attempted to make this happen.

Jesus seems to be the only one to be able to walk on water. We need help to stay on top of the water. This means we either have to make a boat or find something else to make it even possible.

How amazing would it have been to see Jesus walk on water? Some of them thought he was a ghost. However, he was a real person and we can be thankful for the many wonderful miracles that he did.

Talk About It: What do you think it would be like to walk on water? Is this something you would want to do?

Activity: Have everyone make a boat out of paper. Then do a contest to see whose boat floats the longest.

Prayer: You are an amazing God. Thank you for being who you are. Amen.

Then he spit on the ground, made mud with the saliva, and spread the mud over the blind man's eyes.

- John 9:6

Gross! He spits on the ground and makes mud and then puts it on someone's eyes. It seems like this didn't bother anyone else, and maybe Jesus liked to play in the mud. Many today do mud runs and jump through obstacles while getting all dirty to win a race.

However, Jesus wasn't being a part of a mud run. I'm sure he could have even found a cleaner way to heal a blind man's eyes, but for some reason, he chose to spit in the mud. At the same time, it got everyone's attention.

The crowd was watching as Jesus did this. They witnessed a miracle that could not be denied. Everyone would have been able to celebrate and give praise to God for what he did in the mud.

Talk About It: Has God done a miracle in the family? Share it and give praise to God for it.

Activity: Participate in a mud run. If there isn't one in your local area or one that you can go to, make one and have some fun as a family.

Prayer: We praise you for both the gross and the clean miracles you do. Thank you, God. Amen.

GRAB THE EGG

Jesus told her, "I am the resurrection and the life. Anyone who believes in me will live, even after dying.

Ever wonder why people do easter egg hunts? What does an egg have to do with Jesus? Even a little crazier, bunnies don't lay eggs. However, bunnies and eggs are symbols of new life and that is what Jesus is talking about when he says resurrection.

He is the only one who died and rose again. He was given new life and he invites us to have a new life with him. Now, we, of course, don't die and then three days later come back to life. Instead, we are invited to live a better life and we can invite others to join us.

So, the next time you see someone doing an easter egg hunt or you see a bunny running through the yard, remember these tell us of a new life that we get to live. It is an amazing one that is worth celebrating and praising God for.

Talk About It: Is the resurrection of Jesus important? If so, why and what would life be like without it?

Activity: Don't wait for easter, have an easter egg hunt.

Prayer: Thank you God for resurrecting your son, Jesus, and giving us new life. Amen.

PRAISE GOD!

Jesus was in the center of the procession, and the people all around him were shouting, "Praise God! Blessings on the one who comes in the name of the Lord!"

- Mark 11:9

Praise God is a phrase you may have heard often. Usually in church and at least one time a year on a day called, Palm Sunday you have probably heard the word Hosanna. The word Hosanna is a fancy way of saying praise God.

On this special occasion, Jesus was riding on a donkey into Jerusalem and everyone was shouting, "Hosanna, Glory to God in the highest." Now whether you say, "Hosanna" or "Praise God" it is important to say it.

Sometimes we can do this with a musical instrument, writing a poem, or even drawing a picture. There are many ways to praise God and it is important to figure out the best way for you to worship him.

Talk About It: Discuss a variety of ways that someone can worship God. What are the ways that the members of the family worship God?

Activity: Are there ways your family can help out during the worship part of your church services? Find out and participate together.

Prayer: We praise you God and give glory to your name. Amen.

TALENTS

To those who use well what they are given, even more will be given, and they will have an abundance. But from those who do nothing, even what little they have will be taken away.

- Matthew 25:29

You are born with talent. Some of you might be good at sports and others have beautiful singing voices. Still, others might be smart at math, while someone else might be good at languages.

We all have a talent and some of us have to discover it. When we discover it, God gives us more. Yet, if someone never discovers it then they never get to use it and for that reason, some people end up wandering through life feeling like they have no purpose.

Know, that you were created with a purpose. Everyone is. Don't be afraid to explore that purpose. To make a difference in the world and ultimately give glory to God for the wonderful talents he gives you.

Talk About It: What talents are represented in the family? Encourage one another in your talents.

Activity: Put on a talent show. Celebrate everyone's talent.

Prayer: You have made us and you have given us talents. Thank you, God. Amen.

WASHING YOUR FEET

Jesus replied, "A person who has bathed all over does not need to wash, except for the feet, to be entirely clean. And you disciples are clean, but not all of you."

- John 13:10

Imagine going to someone's house and they start to wash your feet. How weird and how gross does this sound? We don't do this anymore because we often have shoes and socks and we don't walk everywhere as they did in Jesus' day.

However, their feet were dirty and it was a custom that when you went to someone's house they would wash their feet. Plus, Jesus isn't talking about how we shouldn't have baths; instead, he is focused on how we are supposed to live.

When we do something wrong, we don't have to start over and ask Jesus to be our Saviour again. Instead, we just need to say we are sorry for what we have done. We are already forgiven and therefore Jesus is telling us to work on being better, one day at a time.

Talk About It: How can we overcome our bad habits or the things we have done wrong? Discuss how you can help each other.

Activity: If you feel comfortable, wash each other's feet. Learn about the custom. If not, go as a family and get pedicures. It's a fun experience, even for guys.

Prayer: You have made us clean. We are sorry for the wrong we have done. Help us to remain clean. Amen.

THE LAST SUPPER

As they were eating, Jesus took some bread and blessed it. Then he broke it in pieces and gave it to the disciples, saying, "Take it, for this is my body."

- Mark 14:22

As Christians, God has asked us to remember Jesus' death and resurrection. One of the main ways we do this is in a ceremony called Communion. Every church does it a little bit differently, but they all focus on what Jesus did for us.

By remembering, we can never forget the good that has happened. We are sometimes sad that Jesus had to die, but we also celebrate since he is alive. It can be a confusing time, and we should be thankful for it.

Communion is also a reenactment of the last supper. For Jesus did similar actions and we might not fully do them the same, but we can take the time to reflect on what it might have been like. Knowing that Jesus would have done everything all over again for just one person.

Talk About It: What are your church's beliefs about communion? Take time to talk about the importance of the ceremony.

Activity: Do your small communion service as a family. This can be a very intimate and spiritual experience.

Prayer: Help us God to remember what you have done and be forever thankful. Amen.

WHAT WOULD YOU HAVE DONE?

And one of them struck at the high priest's slave, slashing off his right ear.

- Luke 22:50

It was a dark night when the soldiers came to arrest Jesus. One of the disciples was so mad that before they could reach Jesus, he took his sword and slashed it off his right ear. It was a dramatic moment. What would you have done if you were there when Jesus was arrested?

Jesus took that ear off the ground and placed it back on the soldier's head, and healed him. It was an amazing moment. Would you have done the same thing if you were Jesus? We would like to think so, but it's hard to imagine.

One would have thought they would have let Jesus go after healing the soldier, but they didn't. He was still arrested. He was put on trial and convicted for a crime he did not commit. The crowds even shouted, "Crucify Him!" What would you have done?

Talk About It: What would you have done if you were there?

Activity: Play the what-if game. Write questions down that start with "what if" and answer them.

Prayer: You have set an example for us. To heal instead of fighting. Thank you, God. Amen.

THE GOOD FRIDAY

When Jesus had tasted it, he said, "It is finished!" Then he bowed his head and gave up his spirit.

- John 19:30

Good Friday is a day that we celebrate the death of Jesus. We might ask ourselves, "What is good about it?" Nobody has a party at a funeral and yet this one is different. He said, "It is finished!"

His plan was finally complete. The moment Adam and Eve ate the fruit, God put a plan in motion so that we could have a better relationship with him and now the plan was done. Jesus had completed it.

Before this moment, animals had to be sacrificed and people had to work hard at being perfect. Since nobody is perfect, God allowed Jesus, who is perfect, to take the blame for everything we did wrong. Then he died on our behalf taking away our punishment.

Talk About It: Compare regular funerals to the Good Friday service. Are there ways we can celebrate Good Friday better?

Activity: Bake some hot cross buns. As you do, talk about the importance of the cross.

Prayer: We are sorry that Jesus had to die and we are thankful for being forgiven. Amen.

JESUS HAS RISEN

He isn't here! He is risen from the dead, just as he said would happen. Come, see where his body was lying.

- Matthew 28:6

There is an old saying, "Friday is here, but Sunday is coming!" This is usually said on Good Friday as we already know that Jesus died, but on Sunday he rose again. It is why most Christians go to church on Sunday. It is a weekly celebration of Jesus' resurrection.

Every time you go to church, you celebrate this moment. Without this event happening, there would be no church. The tomb of Jesus is empty and they have never found the body. Jesus is also the only person in history to be able to do this.

This is truly an event that is worth celebrating and we should always be thankful for it. May we always praise God and never take it for granted.

Talk About It: Discuss the importance of the resurrection. Would there be any point in Christianity without it?

Activity: Grow a plant from a seed or get a butterfly kit. A butterfly kit will help kids see a caterpillar become a cocoon and then a butterfly. It's a great way to explain the resurrection of Jesus.

Prayer: We celebrate and thank you God for the resurrection of your son, Jesus. Amen.

And then he told them, "Go into all the world and preach the Good News to everyone.

- Mark 16:15

Have you ever been allowed to go on a mission trip? Hopped on a plane and flew halfway across the world to help do a building project or work in a school. These things can be exciting and Jesus told his disciples and he tells us today to go into all the world and preach the Good News to everyone.

This is our mission, but we don't have to go to another country. We can start in our very own neighbourhood. Someone nearby may need help with a renovation project or someone else could use the assistance of a tutor. Better yet, they may not have heard the Good News.

What Good News? The Good News is that Jesus has made a way for us to know God. We simply just need to believe that what Jesus said was true and be willing to confess it with our mouths. So, what are you waiting for?

Talk About It: Who was the last person your family led to Christ? What are they up to today? Is there a person that you are leading to Christ right now and what can the family do to help?

Activity: Plan an event at your church or in your neighbourhood that will focus on leading people to Christ.

Prayer: Help us Lord to fulfil our calling of preaching the Good News to everyone. Amen.

After saying this, he was taken up into a cloud while they were watching, and they could no longer see him.

- Acts 1:9

Ever wonder why Jesus had to go to heaven? Wouldn't it be so much easier if he stayed on earth? Think of all the people he could heal and the good that he would perform. It would be so amazing to be able to see him and even the disciples stood there watching until they could no longer see him.

Sometimes we feel the same way when someone in our family passes on. It would be better if they could stay, and yet God has prepared this wonderful place called heaven. He wants us to go there and be with Jesus.

It is a place where there is no more sadness and no more pain. A place we can look forward to and when we get there we can be reunited with the people we love and most of all we get to be with Jesus.

Talk About It: What do you imagine heaven is like? Take some time to find out what everyone thinks.

Activity: If there are people in your family that have already gone to heaven, take some time to remember them. Look at some of their photos or maybe even some journals they left behind.

Prayer: Thank you God for the gift of heaven. Amen.

After Jesus

GOD'S GIFT

And everyone present was filled with the Holy Spirit and began speaking in other languages, as the Holy Spirit gave them this ability.

- Acts 2:4

After Jesus went to heaven, he gave us the gift of the Holy Spirit. Someone who lives inside of everyone who believes in Christ. He speaks to us and helps us to do good, plus he gives us gifts to make us better people.

However, a gift is only good as long as the person continues to use it. Maybe you got something for your birthday or Christmas and you were excited about it for about two weeks. After that, it got put in the closet and was never taken out.

Unless we take the time to learn more about the Holy Spirit and how he works in our life, he will become like that toy sitting around collecting dust. God wants us to blow off the dust of his gift and begin to explore this great life he has given us.

Talk About It: Discuss some thoughts about the Holy Spirit. Would you like to know more?

Activity: As a family spend a month or two praying for more of the Holy Spirit in your lives and see what he does.

Prayer: God, give us more of the Holy Spirit in our lives. Amen.

THE CRIPPLED BEGGAR

Peter said, "I don't have any silver or gold for you. But I'll give you what I have. In the name of Jesus Christ the Nazarene, get up and walk!"

- Acts 3:6

Have you ever seen someone sick in the hospital and prayed for them to get better? Maybe they did, but maybe they didn't. In this case, the person didn't even go to the hospital. They never even expected to get better. They had lost all hope and merely begged for money.

Peter was one of the first leaders in the church and he decided to give the gift of healing instead of money. So he prayed for the person to get better and they did! The person got up and walked!

A story like this should give us hope. God still wants to heal people and he is looking for people who are still willing to pray and believe, just like Peter did.

Talk About It: Do you believe that God still heals? Why or why not? Also, discuss why you think some people are healed and others are not.

Activity: Begin to pray for someone to be healed. Maybe even mark the day you started and then mark the day when the person got healed.

Prayer: Bring healing to our lives and help us to see and give you praise for the miracles you do. Amen.

BOLDNESS

Peter, filled with the Holy Spirit.
- Acts 4:8

Are you a shy person? Avoid large crowds? Maybe you are the opposite. You have no problem talking to people. You can go around and visit everyone in the room. The great thing is, God made us all different and he gives us different kinds so boldness.

Peter was filled with the Holy Spirit numerous times in the Book of Acts, and he wasn't the only one. Each of the people was given exactly what they needed at the right moment. Plus God knew each person and how they acted because he created them.

So he partnered with them by filling them with the Holy Spirit. Therefore, it doesn't matter if you are shy or not. He will give you the boldness you need when you need it. We just need to be willing to surrender to him and let God work in our lives.

Talk About It: What is each personality in your family? Are you thankful that you were created differently? What can you do differently from the rest of everyone else?

Activity: What is your favourite food? Spend a few days preparing meals together and each day prepare someone else's favourite food.

Prayer: Thank you for creating us differently. Help us to surrender more of our lives to the Holy Spirit. Amen.

INVITATIONS

The man replied, "How can I, unless someone instructs me?" And he urged Philip to come up into the carriage and sit with him.

It's so exciting to get invitations. Whether they are for a birthday party or maybe even a wedding. We spend time looking forward to the big day and seeing all of our friends and family. And of course, we don't know about the event unless we get that invite.

The same is true when it comes to church. Some people don't feel like they are wanted at church and they are waiting for someone to invite them. Others have received their invitation, but they just weren't ready and now they want someone to invite them again.

We might think it's silly because we know that anyone can come to church, but some people don't know that. Others are waiting to go with their friend because they are nervous. Maybe someone is waiting for you to invite them.

Talk About It: Who was the last person you invited to church? Did they come? Why or why not? Do you think it is silly to invite people to church? If so, why?

Activity: Come up with some creative ways to invite people to church. It can be a traditional card like you would for a party or maybe a social media posting.

Prayer: Guide us to the people we should invite to church. Give us the right words to say. Amen.

MAY WE SEE

So Ananias went and found Saul. He laid his hands on him and said, "Brother Saul, the Lord Jesus, who appeared to you on the road, has sent me so that you might regain your sight and be filled with the Holy Spirit."

- Acts 9:17

Saul was an interesting person. He didn't like Christians so much that he got permission from the government to be able to kill them. God didn't want this to happen so he wanted to make a difference in Saul's life and he made him blind. Now, this seems weird but God also healed him.

When God opened up Saul's eyes, he became a changed man. He could now see that Jesus was a good person and that the Holy Spirit wanted to make a difference in his life. Eventually, Saul changed his name to Paul and he started many churches.

May God help us to see the difference we can also make in the world. Sometimes we become blind by name calling or bullying and God wants us to know that we are better than that. He wants to open your eyes so that you can see the life he has for you.

Talk About It: Discuss the effects of name-calling or putting other people down and why we shouldn't.

Activity: Blindfold someone or have a contest and blindfold half the family and partner with another person to guide them through the house with their voice. See who can guide the best.

Prayer: Open the eyes of our hearts. Help us to see you better. Amen.

MIRACLES!

Turning to the body he said, "Get up, Tabitha." And she opened her eyes! When she saw Peter, she sat up!

- Acts 9:40

Many miracles happened in the Book of Acts. We have a hard time believing them. Even this one, where Peter simply told a woman who had died to open her eyes and she did. She became alive again. She sat up!

Now if God can do that, one would think he could do other miracles and sometimes he does but we don't see it. We look for the big ones and miss the small ones. The one where a baby was born, or even the time you made it home from work safely. You didn't know it, but God may have prevented an accident.

Miracles happen every day. We just have to look for them and pay attention. Take some time to observe and watch how much God truly loves you.

Talk About It: Do you believe miracles happen every day? Take some time to mention the miracles you are aware of.

Activity: As a family begin to make a list of miracles you see throughout the day and the next time you meet for a family meal, show each other your lists.

Prayer: May we see the miracles you make. Amen.

MISSIONARIES

One day as these men were worshiping the Lord and fasting, the Holy Spirit said, "Appoint Barnabas and Saul for the special work to which I have called them."

- Acts 13:2

We see movies all the time with people who have special work to do. They might be spies or superheroes and in some movies, the people aren't real but in other movies, we see doctors and nurses who are real.

God also appoints certain people to do special work and we call them missionaries. They are people who go to faraway places and they help to build churches, feed the hungry, and educate children. Missionaries help people to know that God loves them.

They also depend on people like you to support them. You often see them in church asking for money, but they also ask for your prayers. Without you, they can't do the special work that God has called them to do, and that is special work that you can do to help them.

Talk About It: Do you know of any missionaries that your church or even your family supports? Get an update on what they are doing. If you don't know one, get to know one.

Activity: Plan a mission trip. Doesn't have to be far, but they can be fun and exciting. It's also a great way to bond as a family.

Prayer: Help us to see the life of a missionary and the special work they do. Amen.

Our Identity In Christ

BLESSED

All praise to God, the Father of our Lord Jesus Christ, who has blessed us with every spiritual blessing in the heavenly realms because we are united with Christ.

Identity has become an important word and it is also important that as Christians we know our identity in Christ. To start, you are blessed. God has blessed you with every spiritual blessing from heaven.

It's like going to a buffet and seeing all the food that is there for us to eat. You could have chicken or beef or pizza or all three. How much we have or what we decide not to have is up to us and it is the same with God. He is offering us spiritual blessings and it is up to us to decide what spiritual blessings we want.

The more we have, the more we have to give. For God doesn't want us to keep our blessings. He wants us to share them with others who are not as blessed.

Talk About It: Has God blessed you and your family? Discuss your blessings and how thankful you are.

Activity: Is there something in your house that you can share with someone else? Does someone else need it more than you? Find out and donate the item or items.

Prayer: Thank you for blessing us. Amen.

UNITED

But now you have been united with Christ Jesus. Once you were far away from God, but now you have been brought near to him through the blood of Christ.

- Ephesians 2:13

Have you ever noticed when there is an earthquake or a hurricane that, people unite together to help the people who have lost their homes or even people they loved? The world is united with compassion in times of trouble.

The saying goes that many hands make light work. This is so true. Therefore people need to come together to make a difference and that is why God made a way for us to be united with Jesus.

God saw us far away from him and heading to a place that would hurt us, so he wanted to help you by making you united with Jesus. By doing this, God can help you in times of trouble and place you in a church, where a group of people can unite and be there when you need it.

Talk About It: What is your church like? Do they come together in times of trouble? Mention a moment when they made a difference in your life or the community.

Activity: Have a three-legged race. Find out the importance of working together to win.

Prayer: Continue to unite us as one group of people willing to work together to help others. Amen.

LOVED

And may you have the power to understand, as all God's people should, how wide, how long, how high, and how deep his love is.

- Ephesians 3:18

People sometimes seek love in all the wrong places and it is because they don't feel loved. We longed to be loved differently and none of us is the same and yet we must realize that God loves us. He is also able to do so in a way that makes you feel like you are loved.

Sometimes we feel loved when our parents get us gifts and others might feel loved when they get a hug from someone else. God however wants us to know that his love is wider, longer, higher, and deeper than you can ever imagine.

His love included giving up his one and only son so that he could get to know you better. Imagine giving up something important for someone else just so you could be with them. That's love and God did that for you.

Talk About It: Discuss the sacrifice that God made for us. How special does that make you feel and why?

Activity: Find out everyone's love language. Take the quiz online and then learn the great ways that you can love the members of your family.

Prayer: We praise you God for loving us and thank you for giving up your son to show it. Amen.

SET APART

Even before he made the world, God loved us and chose us in Christ to be holy and without fault in his eyes.

- Ephesians 1:4

When everything was formless and empty. While the darkness still covered the deep waters God loved you and he chose you. Think about that for a moment. Before the creation of the world, he knew who you were and he still chose you for a purpose.

That purpose is to be holy which is a fancy word for being set apart. Much like a library is set apart to carry books and a pizza shop is set apart to make pizzas, you are set apart to be holy, to partner with God and to share in that love that he has for you.

Not only that but if you were the only person on the planet who needed the love of God, he would still choose you. He would find you and he would still do everything he possibly could to help you be faultless in his eyes.

Talk About It: How does it make you feel to know that before the creation of the world God was thinking about you? Discuss the importance of being set apart.

Activity: When you put water and vegetable oil in a jar together, they are set apart from one another. Try to stir them together and see what happens. Add food colouring and find out what happens.

Prayer: Thank you God for loving us and choosing us before the creation of the world. Amen.

ADOPTION

God decided in advance to adopt us into his own family by bringing us to himself through Jesus Christ. This is what he wanted to do, and it gave him great pleasure.

- Ephesians 1:5

All of us have a birthday, which means we get to celebrate the day we were born. Very few of us get the special honour of having an adoption day. A day when someone else chooses us and makes us a part of their family; however, everyone that chooses to follow God is adopted.

The great thing about adoption is that the people who find the child want to be their parents. They may make a special effort to seek someone out and to make them a part of their family. On top of that, our scripture verse says that it gave God great pleasure to do it.

There is lots of excitement and joy on the day when parents bring home a baby or a child from the adoption home. It is the same with God. The Bible says that even the angels rejoice when each person is welcomed into God's family.

Talk About It: Do you know anyone that was adopted? Take a moment to think about all the different ways adoption is extra special.

Activity: Tour a pet shelter and ask questions about pet adoption. Volunteer a day to help them or make a donation.

Prayer: We are so glad to be adopted into the family of God. Thank you. Amen.

YOU MAKE GOD HAPPY

May you experience the love of Christ, though it is too great to understand fully. Then you will be made complete with all the fullness of life and power that comes from God.

- Ephesians 3:19

You make God happy. Some people need to reread that. You make God happy. No matter what you have done. Maybe you lied about doing your homework or maybe you even stole something from the store. God might not like what you did, but you still make him happy.

That is the hard part of understanding. None of us is perfect and we all make mistakes, but we still make God happy. He still wants you to experience the love of Christ. There also isn't anything that you could do wrong for him to stop.

Take the time to enjoy the experience by worshipping him and talking to him. We will never fully understand how or why we make God happy, so we may as well be thankful that he is.

Talk About It: How can we continue to make God happy? List the many ways.

Activity: Out of the list you made in the Talk About It section, choose one or two for this week and truly continue to make him happy.

Prayer: Help us Lord to continue to make you happy and thank you for making us complete. Amen.

GRACE FILLED

Now all glory to God, who is able, through his mighty power at work within us, to accomplish infinitely more than we might ask or think.

- Ephesians 3:20

Did you ever watch Toy Story? Remember Buzz Lightyear and his famous phrase? "To infinity and beyond!" That word infinity means there is no end and God has filled us with so much grace that we can say, "To infinity and beyond!"

With the help of God and when we are doing what he wants us to do, we can do more than we might ask or think. That is the great thing about being filled with the grace of God. It's kind of like when you hear your parents or your teachers say, "You can become whatever you want."

God is saying the same thing to you. He is giving you special gifts to be able to become whatever you want. You are a grace-filled person and you can go to infinity and beyond.

Talk About It: What do you want to do for God? Do you think it is possible? How hard is it to completely understand the infinity and beyond concept?

Activity: Movie Night with the Family. Watch Toy Story or another movie of your choosing. Get the popcorn out and have some fun.

Prayer: God, we thank you for filling us with your grace and helping us go to infinity and beyond. Amen.

GOD SECURES YOU

Furthermore, because we are united with Christ, we have received an inheritance from God, for he chose us in advance, and he makes everything work out according to his plan.

- Ephesians 1:11

When we go to a bank and we give the teller our money, it is the person's job to make sure that money is safe. They might put it in a drawer and later on in the day they will probably take that money and put it in a safe.

God has done the same thing for you. He is securing your future and he is building an inheritance for us and at the right time, he will give it to you. We might want it now, but God is working everything out according to his plan.

He is waiting for as many people as possible to share in this inheritance. That's how big it is and that is how great it is. God is securing your future and it goes beyond anything we can see right now.

Talk About It: Discuss the concept of inheritance and the idea of heaven.

Activity: If you haven't already, open a savings account for your child(ren) or even the whole family. Use it as a way to demonstrate future security.

Prayer: You have secured our future with great things in store for us. Thank you. Amen.

SHOWERED

He has showered his kindness on us, along with all wisdom and understanding.

- Ephesians 1:8

Ever wondered why we are to shower after we go swimming? The water seems pretty clean and most times after swimming we feel clean. However, we are told we need to shower after swimming to get rid of chlorine or any other things that might be in the water.

We can't see these things but if left on us for long periods, we might get what is called an infection. And God showers us with kindness because he wants to get rid of all the anger and hurt that we might find in the world.

At the same time notice that he gives us wisdom and understanding since we don't know why someone might want to hurt another person. So the next time you take a shower just remember God is showering you with kindness.

Talk About It: How important do you think it is to stay clean? At the same time discuss how important it is to keep our mind focused on good and kind activities.

Activity: If you can go for a day at the beach or a swimming pool. Indoor or outdoor, it doesn't matter. Have fun as a family.

Prayer: As we shower under your kindness, help us to keep our minds on the good in this world. Amen.

YOU HAVE A BIRTHRIGHT

The Spirit is God's guarantee that he will give us the inheritance he promised and that he has purchased us to be his own people. He did this so we would praise and glorify him.

- Ephesians 1:14

We already talked about inheritance and the importance of saving for the future. Now we hear why God has done this for us. He wants us to praise and glorify him, to which we often think of the songs we sing and the prayers we say. However, there are so many ways we can praise God.

Do you have the gift of making pictures? Maybe you like to write. What is the one thing you enjoy doing? Is there a way to make that activity that praises and glorifies God? Did you know God wants to be a part of all the things you like to do?

There are so many ways we can include God and we should want to because we have a birthright. God is securing our future and we should want him to be with us in the present.

Talk About It: Answer the questions in the devotional and discover the different ways God can be praised and glorified within the family.

Activity: Each person in the family can share their gift of praise to God so that everyone can glorify him.

Prayer: Today God, may you be glorified in all we do. Amen.

God's Armour

BELT OF TRUTH

Stand your ground, putting on the belt of truth…

- Ephesians 6:14

The purpose of a belt is to hold the pants up. Without that belt, we might discover the colour of dad's underwear and nobody wants to know that. However, we can also say the same thing about the belt of truth.

People want to know the truth and we need to speak the truth. If we don't then people will discover something they don't want to know about. We call that lies or false ideas.

The only way we can put on the belt of truth is to always be reading the Bible. We can't tell the truth if we don't know it, so every single day, let's make an effort to read the truth.

Talk About It: How important is it, to tell the truth? Discuss the importance of reading your bible every day.

Activity: Play two truths and a lie. Everyone has to say two truths and a lie about themselves and then the family must decide which one is the lie.

Prayer: Help us God to read about the truth and not be afraid to share it with others. Amen.

BUY UNDER ARMOUR

...and the body armour of God's righteousness.
- Ephesians 6:14

Today, under armour is expensive and it is made out of a special fabric that helps keep us dry. Originally the famous sports equipment company intended for their clothing to be worn underneath the athletic jersey. However, many now wear these comfortable pieces of clothing everywhere they go.

God's body armour should be much the same for us. A piece of fabric that keeps God's righteousness with us everywhere we go. Maybe even with a flashy logo that shows that we are a part of his wonderful family.

This helps us to be mindful of others around us. When we put on God's body armour of righteousness, we should want to serve others and extend a loving hand to them. It is an important piece of clothing we should want to wear every day.

Talk About It: Discuss the idea of righteousness as a way of being humble and caring for others. How can we put on the body armour of God's righteousness?

Activity: Make personalized t-shirts with markers or other craft supplies. Maybe even design a flashy logo for the family.

Prayer: Remind us God to put on your armour of righteousness every day. Amen.

PEACEFUL SHOES

For shoes, put on the peace that comes from the Good News so that you will be fully prepared.

- Ephesians 6:15

In some countries, parents can't afford to buy their children shoes and the children still go outside and play. Their feet adjust by developing what are called calluses, thick, hardened layers of skin that protect the body, almost like a naturally developing shoe.

These children become fully prepared for whatever they might want to do throughout the day. Now if you are a person who wears shoes, it's hard to go without them. Therefore, we need to be prepared by putting our shoes on and at times we also need to be prepared to share the Good News.

This means we have to put on peace. When someone wants to hurt us, we don't hurt them back. God's peaceful shoes when tied on the right, help us to be fully prepared to share the peace that comes from God's Good News.

Talk About It: Is there peace in the God News? Discuss as a family the peace that is offered by God.

Activity: Donate to a child in need. Maybe even find an organization that gives shoes to children in third-world countries.

Prayer: Help us Lord to tie on our peaceful shoes as we share your Good News. Amen.

SHIELD OF FAITH

In addition to all of these, hold up the shield of faith to stop the fiery arrows of the devil.

- Ephesians 6:16

Captain America has a cool shield that he even throws into the air and it comes back like a boomerang. This isn't what shields are meant to do. Instead, they are supposed to protect us and God wants us to be protected from the fiery arrows of the devil.

This means that he wants us to be protected from anything that might cause us to walk away from him. Now, after everything we have read so far, this seems impossible. God is so good to us and he gives us so many good things; why would anyone want to do anything else?

Unfortunately, sometimes the devil makes another way of living seem better. We might not even realize it until we think it's too late. If that does happen, know that God will always take you back, so don't throw your shield in the air like Captain America. Instead, protect yourself and hold firm to the things of God.

Talk About It: This is a moment to talk about the appeal of drugs and other forms of addiction. At first, they seem harmless and over time they ruin your life.

Activity: Have some fun with a boomerang or even learn how to throw a Frisbee. If you want, even learn the sport of Frisbee Golf.

Prayer: Thank you for providing us with a shield. Remind us to use it. Amen.

FOOTBALL HELMETS

Put on salvation as your helmet…

- Ephesians 6:17

Football helmets are designed to protect players' heads during a game. They reduce the number of head injuries and even what is called a concussion. Concussions cause headaches and problems with thinking. They might even cause someone to fall over due to a loss of balance.

Without these helmets, the players would have a hard time doing their day-to-day activities. God tells us to put on a similar helmet. However, this helmet provides salvation, which is a fancy word for saving our lives. It doesn't protect us from concussions. Instead, it protects us from death.

Now we all die, but when we die we either go to heaven or hell and if we put on God's helmet of salvation, we go to heaven. Therefore, it is important to put on salvation as your helmet and protect yourself for a life that is yet to come.

Talk About It: Discuss the differences between heaven and hell and the importance of salvation. If someone isn't saved in the family, this is the time to ask them if they want to.

Activity: Get a parent to put a shower cap on. Put shaving foam on it and take turns throwing Cheetos or Cheerios onto the foam. See how many you can get on there. Maybe split into teams and make a competition.

Prayer: We thank you God for giving us the gift of salvation. Help us not to take it for granted. Amen.

SWORDS

…and take the sword of the Spirit, which is the word of God.

- Ephesians 6:17

Swords can look cool. They are sharp and they are meant to protect yourself and to cause damage if someone attacks you. Many movies even portray them as a weapon to use to make someone do what you want them to do, but that isn't what God's sword is about.

God's sword is the Bible and God also gave us the gift of free will. People can read the Bible and choose for themselves and therefore this sword is defensive. It's meant to protect. To defend ourselves with the truth and when used right we might be able to convince others about the same truth.

When we attack others with a sword, we only hurt them. If we hurt them enough times, they eventually want nothing to do with you or God. Therefore, we should use our swords wisely and be careful because the word of God is powerful.

Talk About It: Do you know of an example of when the word of God was used to hurt others? Discuss how we can use it to convince others of God's truth.

Activity: Using pool noodles have a sword fight. Make heart-shaped cut-outs with paper and tape them on your chest. Try to protect yourself.

Prayer: Your word is powerful. Help us to use it wisely. Amen.

Attitudes

THE GOLDEN RULE

Do to others whatever you would like them to do to you.

- Matthew 7:12

This is often called the golden rule. It means that this rule explains how we should live our day-to-day life. How do we want others to treat us? We should treat them the same way.

Now, this seems easy to say, but when someone pushes us on the playground, calls us a bad name, or even cuts us off in the traffic, we don't ask how we would like to be treated. Instead, we usually get upset and angry. Our first reaction is usually about wanting to get revenge.

However, we should probably pause, count to ten, and ask how I would like to be treated. By doing this, we make sure that the other person isn't hurt by us. It also gives us a chance to help them later and God could still partner with us when and if it comes time to share the Good News with them.

Talk About It: Life is more about the eternal consequences. Take a moment to explain the difference between eternal and temporary consequences and how important it is to keep eternal in mind when it comes to making our decisions.

Activity: Each one chooses one person you will make an effort to treat better this week. Talk about who and how.

Prayer: Jesus, we pray that you will help us to remember to treat everyone the way we want to be treated. Amen.

LOVE EVERYONE

But I say, love your enemies! Pray for those who persecute you!
- Matthew 5:44

Sometimes it is hard to imagine but has anyone ever punched you or maybe even kicked you? Maybe they were just reacting out of anger and they came and said sorry to you later, but we typically want to fight back.

Now we shouldn't just take a punch. We should defend ourselves and make sure we are well protected by our parents, friends, or sometimes the police. However, God also doesn't want us to be angry with them. Instead, he says to love your enemies. Even pray for them!

Don't go praying that God will strike them with a thunderbolt. We are to pray that God will help them see what they are doing is wrong. Who knows? Maybe that enemy will become your friend and it's all because you didn't punch back and that enemy might become a Christian. How amazing would that be?

Talk About It: How hard is it not to punch back? Discuss ways that could help us not react so quickly and make a difference in the life of an enemy.

Activity: Is there someone in the church, the neighbourhood, at school or at work that is hard to love? Each person thinks of one person and then finds a practical way to love them. Come back together and talk about how it went.

Prayer: Help us Jesus to love everyone. Amen.

DON'T SHOW OFF

But when you give to someone in need, don't let your left hand know what your right hand is doing.

- Matthew 6:3

Nobody likes a show-off and yet we have probably all seen a person who wants all of the attention. When Jesus said this, people were giving to the poor, and while they were doing it they were telling others.

Today, you might see people on the internet or television, and talk about all the money they have and the needy groups to which they are giving that money. We don't think much of it, and to be honest, nothing has changed. People in the past did it and they still do it today.

One might even think, at least they are giving, let them brag. That is true, but God doesn't want us bragging about the good things we do. We shouldn't do good things to get attention or to make people think about how great we are. We should do good things because we love God and we love other people and it's the right thing to do.

Talk About It: Think about someone who is a show-off. What are your thoughts about them? Can you understand why God doesn't want you to be like that?

Activity: As a family decide upon an organization or a person that you will give to. Send whatever you give without them knowing.

Prayer: Jesus, help us to do things to honour you and not to show off. Amen.

TALK TO GOD

But when you pray, go away by yourself, shut the door behind you, and pray to your Father in private. Then your Father, who sees everything, will reward you.

- Matthew 6:6

We should want to talk to God and it doesn't matter when we talk to him. It can be in church, at school, in the workplace or even in your car. However, sometimes when we get along with God, we tell him things that we wouldn't normally say if other people were around to listen.

This is why it is important to talk to God in private. God gets to hear what is really on your heart and mind. Of course, he already knows, but he loves to hear your voice. He wants to be a part of your life. Every part of your life.

So go ahead, pray with your family and your friends, but also go to your bedroom, shut the door, and pray to God by yourself. The great reward that you will get is a better friendship with God.

Talk About It: How can someone get a better friendship with God by talking to him in private? Discuss how we can tell him anything and how that helps us in our friendship with him.

Activity: Individually build a routine of praying to God by yourself. Even keep a journal or a diary of all the prayers that God answers.

Prayer: Thank you God for being our friend. May we become better and closer friends with you. Amen.

DON'T WORRY, BE HAPPY

That is why I tell you not to worry about everyday life—whether you have enough food and drink, or enough clothes to wear. Isn't life more than food, and your body more than clothing?

- Matthew 6:25

"Don't Worry, Be Happy" was a song written by American musician Bobby McFerrin. Before that, it was an expression that became so popular that it was printed on inspirational cards and posters. One could almost say that Jesus started it. Unfortunately, he never actually said, "Don't worry, be happy."

He taught us the idea that we shouldn't worry about if we have enough to eat or drink or even about the clothes that we are going to wear. Yet we still do because we like to eat and we want to look good wherever we go.

However, there are bigger things in life that we should be concerned about. These are the things that it seems God wants us to focus on. To maybe not focus on our food or our clothes and let God be the one to provide for us.

Talk About It: What are the bigger things in life that God wants us to be concerned about? Why?

Activity: Make a list of those concerns that were discussed. Is there one thing out of that list that you as a family can do?

Prayer: We thank you God for providing our needs. Help us not to worry about them. Amen.

FORGIVE

Do not judge others, and you will not be judged. Do not condemn others, or it will all come back against you. Forgive others, and you will be forgiven.

- Luke 6:37

Did you see what that person was wearing today? How dare mom and dad tell me what to do? It's so unfair? I never want to talk to that person ever again!

These are common statements that get spoken without any thought. They are reactions to situations and yet it is so easy to judge another person, condemn someone for their actions, and never forgive someone. However, notice one important thing. You can only be forgiven if you forgive others.

Sometimes we miss that important point. God wants us to forgive others just like he has already forgiven us. Of course, this makes perfect sense. Why should we be forgiven if we are not willing to forgive others? Remember that next time you have a hard time forgiving someone else.

Talk About It: It can be hard to forgive someone and as long as we are working on it, God knows our heart. Discuss the idea of forgiveness and how hard it is to forgive. Then talk about what God gave up to forgive us.

Activity: Take the extra step to learn to forgive someone you might be having a hard time with. Ask the family for help and guidance and work on it together.

Prayer: Help us to forgive as you have forgiven us. Amen.

CHOOSE YOUR OWN ADVENTURE

You can enter God's Kingdom only through the narrow gate. The highway to hell is broad, and its gate is wide for the many who choose that way.

- Matthew 7:13

Have you ever read a choose-your-own-adventure book or played a video game that gave you options? They can be fun and exciting. The best part is, if you die, you get to start over. There are no consequences for your actions.

Life is like that, but there are consequences. The Bible talks about heaven and hell. We also get to choose which one we want to go to when we die. Notice it says, "many who choose that way." God has given us a choice.

We can receive him and his gift of salvation through Jesus, or we can choose hell. Hell comes with the consequence of pain and torture, while heaven is the exact opposite. The choice is up to you. What will you choose?

Talk About It: Discuss some of the differences between heaven and hell. Do you think we have a choice?

Activity: Find a choose-your-own-adventure book or video game. Have some fun as a family and vote on the choices you make.

Prayer: Thank you God for providing the choice of heaven for us. Amen.

STRANGER DANGER

Beware of false prophets who come disguised as harmless sheep but are really vicious wolves.

- Matthew 7:15

You may have heard of the phrase stranger danger. It was used mostly when strangers would drive around offering candy or puppies to encourage children to get inside. Now the world is much different and we have to be careful about strangers on the internet who talk to us in the privacy of our bedrooms.

Stranger danger can also be used in the church and we have to be careful whom we listen to. Just because the person says they are a Christian and they go to church doesn't necessarily mean they speak for God. They might sound good, but if we know our Bible and we listen closely, God will help us to know the difference.

Talk About It: Stranger danger is an important concept both inside the church and outside the church in everyday life. Here is your opportunity to talk about both the dangers of the internet and make sure you listen to the right people in the church.

Activity: Choose one person to make a list of Bible scriptures, but change some of them slightly and see if the others can find out which ones come from the Bible and which ones are made up.

Prayer: God, continue to give us your Holy Spirit to help us decide what is from you and what is not. Amen.

LISTEN

"But Abraham said, 'If they won't listen to Moses and the prophets, they won't be persuaded even if someone rises from the dead.'"

We listen to lots of stuff. Many of us have headphones or earbuds where we can listen to podcasts, music, and almost anything else that we might want. Our world is full of noise and we are constantly listening whether we want to admit it or not.

One could say that we have become careless in what we listen to and we should learn to be more careful. For if we are listening to the wrong people and the wrong music it will be hard to understand or to see a miracle when it happens.

That is what our scripture is talking about today. The people wouldn't listen to Moses or the words he wrote down for them before he passed away. If they don't listen to him, then they will have an even more hard time believing in miracles.

Talk About It: What are you listening to? Do you think it is important? Discuss the pros and cons.

Activity: Go to a Christian concert. Listen to the experience and enjoy the moment.

Prayer: May we listen to your word so that we can see your miracles. Amen.

PLANT SEEDS

Listen! A farmer went out to plant some seeds.

- Matthew 13:3

There comes a time of the year when it is time to plant some seeds. When that is done there is a waiting period as the seeds grow into plants and then they produce fruits and vegetables that we can enjoy. But none of this happens if the seed is not planted.

We must do the same thing when it comes to talking about God's Good News. A seed has to be planted as we discuss all that God has done for us. We then pray that the spiritual seed will grow inside the person and that it will produce a Christian.

Another part of the Bible talks about how the harvest is plenty but the workers are few. Would you be willing to be a worker today? To help plant seeds and find the harvest.

Talk About It: Take time to discuss the similarities between farming and evangelism. How important do you think it is to participate in evangelism?

Activity: Go to an evangelistic service or watch an evangelical campaign on television. Invite friends to come with you. Maybe take the extra step and volunteer.

Prayer: Just as Jesus did his part by dying on the cross, help us to do our part in reaching the lost. Amen.

HAVE FAITH

If you had faith even as small as a mustard seed, you could say to this mulberry tree, 'May you be uprooted and be planted in the sea,' and it would obey you!

- Luke 17:6

Have you ever seen a mustard seed? It's the smallest of all seeds and yet a mustard tree can grow to be twenty feet or six meters tall. Amazing how something so small could grow to be so big and yet God tells us if we have the faith of the smallest seed in the world then we can experience miracles.

Too often we focus on the size of the matter, when God is saying, "I just want you to have faith. Faith to believe in the impossible." For God is the God of the impossible and he is willing to work in your life if you are willing to have faith.

Sounds easy, but it can be a challenge to learn how to have faith. Start small, and move your way up. Take the time for faith to grow within, for just like the mustard seed, our faith needs to grow over time.

Talk About It: Is faith a process that takes time? What kind of miracles are you hoping to see?

Activity: Start with a small prayer as a family. Continue to pray for it until it comes true. When that happens move on to something bigger and watch as your faith gets bigger like the mustard tree.

Prayer: Give us the gift of faith and may we experience the joy of miracles in our life. Amen.

TURN TO GOD

We had to celebrate this happy day. For your brother was dead and has come back to life! He was lost, but now he is found!

- Luke 15:32

Have you ever lost something? Maybe even searched for days, weeks, or even months and yet you could not find it. Then when you least expect it, all of a sudden it appears. How happy you are when you have finally found it?!

The same is true for God. Now he didn't lose someone. He knows where everyone is at all times. When we say someone is lost, we mean that they are not following God. Instead, they have decided to walk away from him.

Not everyone continues this way. Sometimes they decide to turn toward God and become a Christian. When this happens we say they are found and we celebrate. It is a happy day because the person was lost, but now they have turned to God and they are found.

Talk About It: Do you know of someone who was lost and found? Maybe it was you. Share your story or the story of someone else with the family.

Activity: Hides portions of today's scripture verse throughout the house. Have everyone else look for it and celebrate when all the pieces have been found.

Prayer: Today, we celebrate that we have been found. Help us find others and bring them to you. Amen.

The Future

MEETING JESUS IN THE AIR

Then, together with them, we who are still alive and remain on the earth will be caught up in the clouds to meet the Lord in the air. Then we will be with the Lord forever.

- 1 Thessalonians 4:17

We know that Jesus was on the earth and that he ascended into heaven. The Bible also tells us that he will return and that we will meet him in the air. This has been often referred to as the rapture.

Nobody knows for sure when this will happen but we have the hope that one day, those of us who are still alive, will get the joy of meeting Jesus in the air. It is a hope that we look forward to because it means God is about to change the world and make it the way he intended it to be.

Talk About It: Discuss the idea of the rapture and what parts of the end times you are looking forward to.

Activity: Many books address this issue. For example, the Left Behind Series for Kids. Take the opportunity to research and read and take the time to learn about the rapture and what it means.

Prayer: We look forward to your coming. Thank you, God, for giving us hope. Amen.

HE'S COMING AGAIN

Look! He comes with the clouds of heaven. And everyone will see him

- Revelation 1:7

The Bible also talks about a day when Jesus will physically come to earth again. Just like when the disciples watched Jesus go up into heaven, people will see him come down from heaven. Notice the scripture says everyone will see him.

People have often wondered how everyone will see him but today with our modern technology, we will be able to see this wonderful event through our phones, on our computers, and on television. People from all over the world will get a chance to see Jesus come down from heaven.

We can also look forward to this wonderful day. For it is a day when Jesus will take over and make our world a better place. Our cares and our worries will be gone. The hope that we are looking for will be made complete.

Talk About It: Take the time to imagine what this day will look like. Do you think some will be surprised or is it possible that many will be ready?

Activity: Be creative. Pretend you are a reporter when Jesus returns to earth. How would you report the scene? Describe what you think they will say.

Prayer: Thank you Jesus for your promise that you will return. We believe you. Amen.

BE READY

However, no one knows the day or hour when these things will happen, not even the angels in heaven or the Son himself. Only the Father knows.

- Matthew 24:36

Ever had to get ready for a big event? Maybe a wedding. Everyone spends months preparing. Brand-new suits are purchased while the women try on dresses and spend what seems like forever accessorizing.

For a wedding, we know what day it is going to happen and we can get ready. How do you get ready for an event that you don't know when it will be? This seems impossible and yet we should try every day to be ready with excitement.

This might not be the day that Jesus returns, and we can spend most of it trying to help others become Christians. That is how we get ready by helping others to be ready. Besides, you wouldn't want them to go to a wedding without their best clothes, and you should also want them to be ready for when Jesus returns.

Talk About It: What are some other ways we can be ready for Jesus' return? Make a list and see what you can come up with.

Activity: As a family, help get ready for a big event. What is needed? How can each family member help?

Prayer: Help us to be ready for your return Jesus. Also, help us to help others. Amen.

EVERYTHING MADE NEW

Then I saw a new heaven and a new earth, for the old heaven and the old earth had disappeared. And the sea was also gone.

- Revelation 21:1

Ever hurt your knee trying to learn how to ride a bike? Maybe you have had to go to a funeral for someone in your family. The great thing about the return of Jesus is that we no longer have to experience pain, and we no longer have to watch people die. All of these things will disappear.

These are just a couple of reasons why we look forward to Jesus' return. For he makes the old heaven and the old earth disappear. He will create a new heaven and a new earth where there will be no more pain, no more tears, and no more death.

How wonderful of a life that will be! We often wonder why we have to wait, but Jesus is waiting for the very last person to become a Christian so that as many people as possible can experience life on the new earth. How great it will be!

Talk About It: Imagine life with no hospitals, funeral homes, or pharmacies. That is just a glimpse of the new earth. Discuss what else you think it will look like.

Activity: Create something new. Maybe something out of wood. Possibly a fort in the backyard. Do it as a family.

Prayer: We look forward to the day when everything will be made new. Thank you, God, for all you are doing. Amen.

SEX!

Give honour to marriage, and remain faithful to one another in marriage. God will surely judge people who are immoral and those who commit adultery.

- Hebrews 13:4

Guess what?! God created sex! He created it for marriage. During the time of Jesus, when a man and a woman got married, they put up a tent in the middle of the celebration and the husband and wife went into the tent to have sex while everyone was celebrating outside the tent.

He didn't want us to have sex before that moment. He also didn't want us to have sex with another person after that moment. It was just meant for two people together for the rest of their lives. They could have sex as much as they wanted as long it was with just the two of them. Studies have also shown that when sex is done the way God intended it to be, it is more enjoyable and more fulfilling. So, why look for something second-hand when you can have the real deal?

Talk About It: Discuss the importance of sex with just a husband and wife.

Activity: Do some research on sexually transmitted diseases and discover the importance of having sex with just one person for life.

Prayer: Help us God to discover your true will in creating sex for us. Amen.

I MESSED UP

But if we confess our sins to him, he is faithful and just to forgive us our sins and to cleanse us from all wickedness.

- 1 John 1:9

Maybe it's too late. You have already had sex outside of marriage. What does one do now? You confess it, especially to God. For when we do that he is faithful to forgive us and cleanse us. Some people even believe that if we do this we become born-again virgins.

The reality is, it's not too late to become faithful again. Our God is the God of second chances. If needed, there can be a third or a fourth. What is important is that you are trying to be better. You are trying to avoid the temptations.

By doing all you can to change your life, you show God that you are being faithful to him. So if you have messed up, it's okay. It's never too late to turn to him and confess what you have done and start all over again.

Talk About It: Has your teenager had sex? The important thing here is to not yell or act upset. Even promise you won't and be prepared for the day when they confess. By not yelling at them, you will open the doors to a deeper relationship with your teenager and you can help them with their temptations.

Activity: Continue to build that deeper relationship with them and take them somewhere they want to go and participate with them.

Prayer: If and when I mess up, help me to be quick to confess. Amen.

DATING AND STARBUCKS MENUS

Who can find a virtuous and capable wife? She is more precious than rubies.

- Proverbs 31:10

In the world of Tinder and Bubble, it can be hard to find someone you want to spend the rest of your life with. It could feel like you are going to a Starbucks for the very first time. Especially when a tall is their smallest, a grande is technical a medium and not a large, plus venti means twenty but the cup size is only 16 ounces.

None of it makes sense and neither does the dating world. Everyone struggles with it and modern technology has not helped us. It has only given us more options to explore. The more options we have the harder it is to decide.

Try going to a restaurant that has a ten-page menu. It takes longer to decide and it would be nice if we could try a little bit of everything to decide. Guess what?! That's what the dating world has become. Let me try a little bit of everything when God only intended me to have one.

Talk About It: Do you agree with this analogy? Why or why not? What can we do to make it simpler to find the person we want to spend the rest of our life with?

Activity: Is your teenager already dating someone? Take the time to get to know the other person. Invite them over for dinner. Make them feel welcome in your home.

Prayer: In a world full of decisions help us to make the right ones. Amen.

TRUE LOVE?

Love is patient and kind. Love is not jealous or boastful or proud.

A person can love pizza and a wife can love a husband. Both words mean two different kinds of love. There is a love to describe affection for an object and a love towards a person. At the same time, there is a love that a person can have for a friend and then there is the lustful love that makes us want to have sex with the person.

The question is, what is true love? The answer is, all of them. However, I think we need to reword the question. Instead of looking for true love, maybe we should ask what the greatest love is and how it looks.

1 Corinthians talks about it being patient and kind. Not jealous or boastful, however, John 15:13 says, "There is no greater love than to lay down one's life for one's friends." Jesus did that for us and that might be the greatest example of love for us that we can find.

Talk About It: What does true love look like to you? Is there someone or something that you are looking for? Is it possible to find love with Jesus?

Activity: Take the time to use 1 Corinthians 13 to discover what love looks like and then ask how this can be applied today.

Prayer: Thank you Jesus for giving us an example of the greatest love. Help us to better define it. Amen.

FRIENDS WITH BENEFITS?

Now the man and his wife were both naked, but they felt no shame.

- Genesis 2:25

Friends with Benefits was a movie in 2011 with Justin Timberlake and Mila Kunis. It hasn't been a new concept and it can be appealing to some. To have all the fun of sex without the emotional attachment. The problem is when two people come together sexually, they form a bond both physically and spiritually.

Weirdly, you can say they become married and yet they are not. The two people begin to form emotions for each other even though they are agreed not to. A friends-with-benefits situation may work for a time but it will eventually break down and people will get hurt.

Why? It wasn't the way God designed us. He brought Adam and Eve together and when they were both naked they felt no shame because they were two people with a close bond. A bond that is greater than any friendship.

Talk About It: Discuss some of the sexual relationships that are happening in high school. There are all sorts of situations that God never intended. Why do we think that is?

Activity: Find out the best way to help your teenager through the middle or high school years. Have an open conversation. Remember, no yelling, don't get angry, just listen.

Prayer: You created Adam and Eve with a purpose. Thank you, God, for giving us an amazing example. Amen.

GOD THINKS YOU'RE THE BEST

Others were given in exchange for you. I traded their lives for yours because you are precious to me. You are honoured, and I love you.

- Isaiah 43:4

Reread that scripture. Let it sink in. Read it slowly. Others were given in exchange for you. I traded their lives for yours because you are precious to me. You are honoured, and I love you.

I can name one particular person who was traded for you. Jesus, God's only son. He traded his life for yours because you are precious to him. You matter to him. You are honoured, and God loves you.

As life gets harder and harder you need to hear that. With suicide and addictions on the rise, you need to hear that you matter. God thinks you are the best. Not only does God think you are the best, but so do your parents, many of your friends, and many more. Don't give up. Don't ever give up, for God thinks you are the best.

Talk About It: Discuss the topic of suicide and mental health. Has anyone close to you died by suicide? How can we make a difference?

Activity: Contact a suicide hotline or a mental health support group and find out how you can help make a difference.

Prayer: Thank you God for trading Jesus' life for mine. We are honoured and we love you in return. Amen.

GOD HAS A PLAN FOR YOUR LIFE

For I know the plans I have for you," says the Lord. "They are plans for good and not for disaster, to give you a future and a hope.

- Jeremiah 29:11

We often see Jeremiah 29:11 at graduation celebrations because it is true. Young people don't often know what the next step is. They are usually just going to college or university because that is what was taught to them. It's the next step in life so I might as well do it and make the best of it.

Wandering around without a plan or a purpose isn't good. Yet, God has a plan for everyone. It's a good one that gives us a future and hope. The problem is we often listen to our guidance counsellor and even parents have good advice, but sometimes it isn't God's plan.

As graduation times approached it is a time when we should be going to our private bedrooms, shutting the door, and asking God what his plan for our life is. Then we should listen. Let him dictate the next steps. Not the world.

Talk About It: Do you have a plan? Is it God's plan? How can we know the difference?

Activity: Take some time alone to discover God's plan for your life. Don't rush the process, but learn to sit and wait upon the Lord.

Prayer: Allow your plan and your purpose for our lives to come to the surface. Amen.

DON'T GIVE UP

So let's not get tired of doing what is good. At just the right time we will reap a harvest of blessing if we don't give up.

- Galatians 6:9

This verse is often used in church settings for moments when it seems that all is lost. Nobody new is coming but we shouldn't give up. God will give us the harvest at just the right time, but young people, you shouldn't give up either.

It's so easy to just throw your hands up in the air and say that my marks don't matter, the school doesn't matter, and neither does my life. I'm not going to make a difference in this world. As long as we keep saying that to ourselves, we won't make a difference.

Thomas Edison invented the incandescent lightbulb but it took him one thousand unsuccessful attempts. He failed one thousand times. When asked how it felt to fail so many times, he said, "I have not failed - I've successfully found many ways that will not work."

Just because you don't succeed the first time, keep trying. Don't give up.

Talk About It: What hurts the most about failure? How can we overcome this?

Activity: Find something hard to accomplish and see if there is a way to overcome it.

Prayer: Help us Lord not to give up. Give us the encouragement we need to keep going. Amen.

I'M BORED

Don't let anyone capture you with empty philosophies and high-sounding nonsense that come from human thinking and from the spiritual powers of this world, rather than from Christ.

- Colossians 2:8

Did you know that boredom is an emotional sign that you are doing something that doesn't give you satisfaction? It happens when you have low levels of dopamine in the brain. It is also why we go to social media a lot. Social media helps us to get a quick fix of dopamine. Unfortunately, it doesn't last long and we get bored again.

Social media has become our empty philosophies and high-sounding nonsense that comes from human thinking and from the spiritual powers of this world. It can be an amazing tool if used right, but for the most part, we don't. We need to be careful because social media can become addictive.

Before we know it, we might find all of our answers on another platform instead of the Bible. The boredom we feel could lead us to a source of our strength that is not in Christ. Therefore watch what you are looking at and be careful of what you listen to.

Talk About It: What social media platforms are you using? Discuss the differences and why it is important to control social media before it controls you.

Activity: Participate in a social media fast for at least 30 days and see if there is a difference in your life.

Prayer: Strengthen us as we seek you above everything else. Amen.

TALK TO YOUR PARENTS

Confess your sins to each other and pray for each other so that you may be healed. The earnest prayer of a righteous person has great power and produces wonderful results.

We end with this because it is probably the most important aspect of being in a family. Talking to your parents. We need someone that we can go to at all times. Someone we can confess to you without fear. Someone we know that will help us.

Throughout this section, there has been a warning to the parents. Don't yell at your kids or get angry with them when they come to you with sensitive issues. It may be disappointing, and you expect better from them, but you need to be there to help them and the young people. You need them.

Therefore, make your relationship one where you can confess to your parents so that they can pray for you and they can help you heal. Your parents will be able to pray for you and expect wonderful results as you turn to them and God.

Talk About It: Discuss what needs to happen to make your relationship more open.

Activity: Work on deepening your relationship as a family.

Prayer: Thank you God for giving us each other and placing us in the family that you have created. Amen.